REIGNITING THE FIRE OF SOUL WINNING IN OUR CHURCHES

Pastor Dr. Claudine Benjamin

REIGNITING THE FIRE OF SOUL WINNING IN OUR CHURCHES.
Copyright @ 2025. Pastor Dr. Claudine Benjamin. All rights reserved.

For more information or to book an event, contact:
inspiredtowinsouls@gmail.om

No part of this publication may be reproduced, stored in a retrieval system or transmitted in any form or by any means, electronic, mechanical, photocopying, recording or otherwise without the prior written permission of the author.

Portions of this book include content adapted from The Great Commission Connection by Dr. Raymond Culpepper. Used with permission. All rights reserved.

Published by:

Editor: Cleveland O. McLeish (Author C. Orville McLeish)

ISBN: 978-1-965635-46-9 (paperback)

Unless otherwise stated, all Scripture quotations are taken from the King James Version (KJV).

Scripture quotations marked "KJV" are taken from the Holy Bible, King James Version (Public Domain).

DEDICATION

To every pastor, leader, and believer who refuses to let the fire for lost souls go out.

This book is dedicated to those who labor in the shadows, weep in the secret place, and burn with a passion to see the kingdom of God multiply through the salvation of men. May your fire never be extinguished, and may your reward be eternal.

To every pastor who has stood behind pulpits—faithfully preaching not for popularity, but for repentance.

To every leader who has wept in secret over the spiritual condition of their city, longing to see souls come to Christ.

To every believer who has dared to leave comfort behind and obey the call to *"go out into the highways and hedges, and compel them to come in."*

To the nameless intercessors who carry the burden for the lost in prayer, night after night, when no one is watching.

To the outreach teams who show up in neighborhoods most would avoid, with nothing in their hands but a tract and the fire of the gospel in their hearts.

To those who have been ridiculed, misunderstood, or discouraged in their pursuit of soul winning—and kept going anyway.

This book is for you.

May this work serve as both a confirmation and a commission—a confirmation that your labor is not in vain—and a commission to keep the fire burning until every soul has heard, every altar is filled, and every street knows the name of Jesus.

Let it be said of us: we answered the call, we obeyed the mission, and we did not let the fire go out.

This book is dedicated to the burden-bearers, the soul-chasers, the gospel-sharers, and the church-builders.

This is for you—and those you've yet to reach.

ACKNOWLEDGMENTS

To God be all the glory—for the burden, fire, and vision that birthed this book. Every word written was prayerfully crafted with one cry in mind: *"Lord, reignite the church for the harvest."*

I want to express my deepest gratitude to Dr. Raymond F. Culpepper for graciously allowing me to include and adapt portions of his powerful work, The Great Commission Connection. His voice has served as a prophetic trumpet in this generation, calling the church back to its mission with unwavering urgency. Dr. Culpepper, thank you for your faithfulness to the call and for helping to lay a strong foundation that many of us are privileged to build upon.

To my family—thank you for your endless love, patience, and support. Your prayers, sacrifices, and encouragement made space for me to walk out this calling and complete this assignment. I cherish you more than words can express.

To my church family—thank you for being a living example of what it means to carry the gospel with fire. Your hunger, faith, and burden for souls have deeply inspired this work. Thank you for standing with me, praying through the process, and believing in the power of evangelism.

To every intercessor, pastor, teacher, and evangelist who still weep over souls and burn with holy urgency—you are the reason this message still matters. May your fire never die out.

Let this be more than a book. Let it be a spark.

To God be all the glory, now and forever.

ABOUT THE AUTHOR

Pastor Claudine Benjamin is a passionate Kingdom voice, a servant-leader, and a relentless soul-winner committed to advancing the mission of Jesus Christ. With a heart that burns for revival and a voice that cries out for the restoration of the Church's evangelistic fire, she has dedicated her life to proclaiming the gospel, equipping believers, and calling the Church back to its first love.

Her ministry is rooted in bold truth, fervent prayer, and the power of the Holy Spirit. Pastor Claudine has ministered to congregations, communities, and individuals through preaching, teaching, and writing with an anointing that both convicts and ignites. Her message is clear: the harvest is still plentiful, the laborers are still few, and now is the time to rise.

Reigniting the Fire of Soul Winning in Our Churches is more than a book—it is a prophetic charge to the Body of Christ to return to the altar, reclaim the mandate, and reach the lost at any cost. Through every page, Pastor Claudine echoes the heart of heaven and stirs the Church to walk in holy urgency.

She is the author of several other books focused on revival, purpose, healing, and discipleship. As a spiritual mentor, prayer warrior, and fire-starter in the Kingdom, her mission remains: to see souls saved, lives transformed, and the Church reignited for the glory of God.

She is a devoted mother of three children and six grandchildren.. She loves her Church family Newlife Church Community Ministries. Her passion is to Win The Lost At All Cost.

TABLE OF CONTENTS

Dedication iii
Acknowledgments v
About the Author vii
Introduction: Why the Fire Must Burn Again 11
Chapter 1: The Forgotten Mandate—Rediscovering the Great Commission 15
Chapter 2: When Evangelism Becomes an Option, Not a Command 21
Chapter 3: Signs the Fire Has Gone Out in the Church 25
Chapter 4: Reigniting Passion in the Pulpit and the Pew 29
Chapter 5: Restoring Evangelism to the Core of Church Culture 37
Chapter 6: Equipping the Saints – Turning Believers into Bold Witnesses 53
Chapter 7: Creating a Culture of Compassionate-Driven Outreach . 61
Chapter 8: Overcoming Fear, Apathy, and Distraction in Evangelism 65
Chapter 9: The Role of Leadership in Modeling the Mission 69
Chapter 10: Practical Strategies to Reignite Evangelism in Your Church 73
Chapter 11: Raising Up a New Generation of Soul Winners 77
Chapter 12: Staying on Fire – Keeping Evangelism at the Heart 81
Chapter 13: Profiles of Impact – Characters of Soul Winning Fire . 85
Chapter 14: The Revival That Starts With Reaching One 99
Chapter 15: Return to the Mission 107

Chapter 16: Return to the Fire 113
Chapter 17: A Call Back to the Fire... 119
Chapter 18: Cry Out for Fresh Fire.. 175
Chapter 19: Rejecting Showmanship – Returning to Authentic Power 207
Chapter 20: A Call to Return 219
Chapter 21: We Are a Sent People 231
Chapter 22: The Church Has Lost the Fire for Soul Winning 235
Chapter 23: A Church on Fire Cannot Be Ignored 245
Chapter 24: The Church on Fire for the Harvest 257
Chapter 25: Rekindling the Flame of Evangelism in the Church ... 263
Chapter 26: When the Fire for Souls Has Gone Out 269
Chapter 27: Holiness.. 283
Chapter 28: Equipping the Church to Overcome and Restore the Soul Winning Fire 295
Chapter 29: Let the Fire Fall Again 303
Chapter 30: Church Activation Checklist: Reigniting the Fire for Soul Winning.. 313
Conclusion: Until the Whole World Hears 317
Reflection Guide 327
A Call to the Church Today 327
Scripture Reference Index.. 329

INTRODUCTION

WHY THE FIRE MUST BURN AGAIN

Something vital is missing in many churches today. The music is excellent, the programs are polished, the preaching is strong—but the fire to reach the lost is flickering, or in some cases, completely gone. The church has become increasingly inward-focused, pouring time and energy into keeping the saved satisfied, while the unsaved slip further away from the reach of redemption.

This book was born out of a holy urgency. Soul winning is not a trend or a niche—it is the very reason the church exists. When we lose our evangelistic fire, we lose our relevance. We were not commissioned to build comfortable gatherings—we were sent to invade darkness with the light of Christ and bring the lost home.

This book is a call to reignite that flame—not just in individuals, but in the entire culture of the local church. It is a roadmap for pastors, leaders, and members who are ready to shift from maintenance to mission.

The fire can burn again. The great commission can become the great priority. The altar can be filled with new believers, not just recycled saints. But it starts with a fresh awakening—a decision to return to what matters most.

Reigniting the Fire of Soul Winning in Our Churches

Why the Fire Must Burn Again

The soul winning fire in many churches has not been extinguished by hatred or rebellion—but by distraction, routine, and the slow drift of cultural compromise. Many local assemblies still gather, worship, and function, yet something vital is missing: the burning urgency to win the lost.

In the early church, evangelism was not a department—it was a lifestyle. Every believer was a witness. Every gathering was an opportunity to equip the saints for outreach. But today, in many places, the fire that once drove the church outward has turned inward. We've moved from urgency to apathy, from pursuit to preservation.

The fire must burn again.

A Church Without Evangelism Is a Church Without Oxygen

Just as a fire dies without oxygen, a church dies without evangelism. No matter how gifted the pastor, how talented the choir, or how excellent the programming—if we are not winning souls, we are not fulfilling our purpose.

> **"The fruit of the righteous is a tree of life; and he that winneth souls is wise."—(KJV)**

We have too many churches with structure, but no soul; crowds, but no conversions; noise, but no new birth. We must ask the hard questions:

Pastor Dr. Claudine Benjamin

- When was the last time someone gave their life to Christ in our services?

- Are we preaching for applause or for salvation?

- Has our Sunday experience replaced our evangelistic mission?

The Fire Doesn't Start with Programs—It Starts with People

Before a church regains its evangelistic power, its people must regain their personal fire for souls. Pastors must preach it. Leaders must model it. Members must live it. Evangelism must not be seasonal—it must be constant.

> **"They that sow in tears shall reap in joy." —Psalm 126:5 (KJV)**

It's not about gimmicks or mass marketing. It's about genuine burden—about tears, compassion, and obedience.

Why This Book Exists

This book is a trumpet blast—a call to realign the church with the mission Jesus left us;not to entertain believers, but to reach the broken; not to build audiences, but to make disciples; not to play church, but to be the church.

The fire has gone out in many places—but it can burn again, and it must.

> **"Where there is no vision, the people perish…"** — **Proverbs 29:18 (KJV)**

This book is about restoring that vision—until your church becomes known not just for what happens inside the building, but for what happens when your people leave it to rescue the lost.

CHAPTER 1

THE FORGOTTEN MANDATE– REDISCOVERING THE GREAT COMMISSION

"Go ye therefore, and teach all nations…" —Matthew 28:19 (KJV)

The great commission is not a suggestion—it's a command. Yet in many churches today, it has become the great omission. Churches host more conferences on church growth than they do calls to repentance. We train greeters, musicians, and hospitality teams, but often neglect to train soul winners.

The mission hasn't changed—but the church has. We've drifted from our assignment to go and tell, and replaced it with a model of come and see. But Jesus didn't die just so we could have better Sunday experiences—He died so that people from every nation, tribe, and tongue could be saved.

What Happened to the Mission?

Somewhere along the way, the church became more focused on seating capacity than sending capacity. We've prioritized programs over people, events over evangelism, and influence over impact. While the buildings grew, the burden for the lost diminished.

Reigniting the Fire of Soul Winning in Our Churches

The great commission has been buried under the weight of routine ministry, but it's time to dig it out, dust it off, and place it back at the center of our churches.

The Mandate Is Not Optional

Jesus didn't give us multiple ministry tracks to choose from. The call to evangelize is for every believer, not just those with a "calling" to missions. Every saved person is a sent person. When we treat soul winning as optional, we create churches filled with consumers, not carriers of the gospel.

We Must Preach the Gospel Again

The gospel is not just about improving lives—it's about rescuing souls. It's not self-help; it's salvation. We must stop softening the message to keep people comfortable. Hell is still real. Heaven is still eternal. Sin still separates. Jesus is still the only way.

When we rediscover the weight and wonder of the gospel, we'll find our voice again.

Let the Commission Become the Culture

To reignite the fire of soul winning in the church, the great commission must become more than a sermon—it must become the culture. Every decision, department, and disciple must carry the question: *"How are we reaching the lost?"*

> **"Go ye therefore, and teach all nations, baptizing them… teaching them to observe all things whatsoever I have commanded you…" —Matthew 28:19–20 (KJV)**

The final words Jesus gave the church were not about comfort, convenience, or community-building. He gave us a mandate—one that transcends centuries, cultures, and denominations: *Go and make disciples of all nations.*

Yet in many churches, this mandate has been marginalized. The great commission has become the great suggestion. It's referenced, quoted, and printed on banners—but too often, it is not practiced.

Mandate, Not Ministry Option

When evangelism becomes one ministry among many, it's easy to treat it like an option rather than the church's central mission. But evangelism was never meant to compete with worship, prayer, or teaching. It is the mission that fuels them all.

> **"How then shall they call on him in whom they have not believed? and how shall they believe in him of whom they have not heard?" —Romans 10:14 (KJV)**

If the lost are not hearing the gospel, they are not believing. And if they are not believing, they are not being saved. The church must re-engage the full weight of this mandate.

Evangelism Is for Everyone

One of the great deceptions in the modern church is that evangelism is the job of pastors or outreach departments. But scripture is clear:

> **"But ye shall receive power, after that the Holy Ghost is come upon you: and ye shall be witnesses..." —Acts 1:8 (KJV)**

Every Spirit-filled believer is a witness. Not everyone is an evangelist by office, but everyone is called to evangelize. To be filled with the Spirit is to be empowered to reach the world.

The Great Commission Is Not Culturally Outdated

Some argue that in today's modern, pluralistic world, direct evangelism feels "aggressive" or "irrelevant." But the gospel has never needed to be edited—it needs to be declared. Culture changes, but truth does not.

> **"For I am not ashamed of the gospel of Christ: for it is the power of God unto salvation to every one that believeth…"**
> **—Romans 1:16 (KJV)**

The church must stop apologizing for its message and start proclaiming it with boldness.

When the Mandate Is Rediscovered, Revival Begins

Churches that rediscover evangelism don't just grow in numbers—they grow in power. Evangelism reawakens compassion, deepens prayer, stirs fasting, and unifies purpose.

> **"…the Lord added to the church daily such as should be saved." —Acts 2:47 (KJV)**

That's the result of a soul winning culture. The church doesn't need a new strategy—it needs to return to the original mandate.

From The Great Commission Connection, Dr. Culpepper wrote: *"One of the most compelling features of Luke 15 is the joy that is manifested when the lost is found. It is amazing that heaven breaks forth in celebration of joy when one lost person is found. Bill Hybels says, "When a sinner is saved, heaven throws a party." The joy alone is enough reason for us to focus on the missional mandate of the church. When the church loses its focus on finding the lost, the joy of the people will sour. The new birth of a soul brings forth the same excitement to the church family as the natural birth of a child brings to an earthly family."*

CHAPTER 2

WHEN EVANGELISM BECOMES AN OPTION, NOT A COMMAND

> "Why call ye me, Lord, Lord, and do not the things which I say?" —Luke 6:46 (KJV)

There is a dangerous mindset creeping into the modern church—one that treats obedience to Christ's call as elective rather than essential. It presents evangelism as a personality-based gift rather than a Spirit-led lifestyle. Slowly, subtly, the great commission is replaced with great convenience.

Jesus didn't ask for suggestions. He gave commands. He didn't say, *"If you're comfortable, share the gospel."* He said:

> "Go ye into all the world, and preach the gospel to every creature." —Mark 16:15 (KJV)

When evangelism becomes an option, it ceases to be urgent. When it ceases to be urgent, souls go unreached.

How Evangelism Becomes Optional

1. **When comfort takes priority over calling,** churches begin to shape services around what makes people stay, rather than what makes them go. The goal becomes attendance, not

assignment.

2. **When silence is safer than truth**, a culture that increasingly rejects moral absolutes feels it is easier to stay quiet than to risk offense. But silence is not love—truth spoken in love is.

3. **When the fear of rejection outweighs the fear of God**, the opinions of people begin to matter more than the eternal consequences of lost souls.

4. **When the church replaces evangelism with activity**, programs increase. Events multiply. But souls aren't being saved. We're doing more—but reaching fewer.

The Cost of Treating Evangelism Lightly

When evangelism becomes a side effort, churches lose:

- Their prophetic voice in the community.
- Their compassion for the broken.
- Their identity as ambassadors of Christ.
- Their fire in the Spirit.

Most tragically, they lose harvest.

> **"The harvest truly is plenteous, but the labourers are few."**
> **—Matthew 9:37 (KJV)**

Why are the laborers few? It is not because people aren't saved but because many saved people have believed the lie that evangelism is optional.

Evangelism Is Not a Spiritual Gift—It's a Spiritual Mandate

It doesn't require a stage, sermon, or spotlight. It requires obedience. You don't need eloquence—you need burden. You don't need a platform—you need availability.

"If ye love me, keep my commandments." —John 14:15 (KJV)

Obedience to Christ includes obedience to His last and most urgent command: *Go and make disciples.*

Restoring Evangelism as a Non-Negotiable

Churches must:

- Reintroduce the great commission in new members classes.
- Train every believer to witness—at home, work, and beyond.
- Embed evangelism into every ministry—not just "outreach teams."
- Celebrate salvations and testimonies regularly.
- Hold believers accountable for spiritual fruit.

This is not just about church growth—it's about kingdom expansion. The church must refuse to reduce evangelism to a personality trait or occasional event—it is the very mission we exist for.

CHAPTER 3

SIGNS THE FIRE HAS GONE OUT IN THE CHURCH

> "Nevertheless I have somewhat against thee, because thou hast left thy first love." —Revelation 2:4 (KJV)

A church can be active without being alive. It can have music, lights, sermons, and people—yet lack the spiritual fire that compels it to reach the lost. The early church burned with urgency. Today, many churches glow with familiarity but have lost their flame.

How can we tell if the evangelistic fire has gone out?

1. Souls are no longer getting saved.

In Acts 2, the church exploded with conversions. Daily, people were being added—not just attendees, but believers.

> "And the Lord added to the church daily such as should be saved." —Acts 2:47b (KJV)

If weeks and months pass without a salvation, something is wrong. A lack of souls is not a sign of a hard harvest—it's a sign of a cold church.

2. Altar calls are missing or mechanical.

The fire of soul winning burns hottest when the message leads to an invitation. But in many pulpits today, altar calls have vanished—or become mere formalities.

When the church loses the urgency of decision, it loses the fire of salvation.

3. Outreach is a department, not a culture.

In churches where the fire has faded, evangelism is relegated to a team, a day, or a monthly event. But in a burning church, everyone is involved. Every service, small group, and ministry radiates a heart for the lost.

Evangelism is not one program among many. It's the fuel for everything else.

4. Testimonies are scarce.

Where the fire is burning, stories abound. Testimonies flow from the pulpit and pew. New believers share how they encountered Jesus. Baptisms are happening. Evangelism is working.

But when the fire dies, so do the stories. Silence replaces celebration. Salvation becomes distant history rather than current reality.

5. Messages are comfortable instead of convicting.

The gospel brings hope, but it also brings conviction. A church that avoids preaching repentance, sin, and eternity has likely traded fire for familiarity.

> **"For the time will come when they will not endure sound doctrine…"** —2 Timothy 4:3a (KJV)

That time has come in many places—and only the fire of truth can break the cycle.

6. Prayer meetings shrink instead of stir.

A soul winning church prays differently. It weeps. It groans. It calls out the names of the lost. But when the fire goes out, prayer becomes mechanical. The burden is gone, and without burden, there is no breakthrough.

It's Not Too Late to Rekindle the Flame

If your church sees these signs—it's not hopeless. It's a wake-up call. The Holy Spirit is ready to reignite the altar. The question is: will we allow Him?

> **"Quench not the Spirit."** —1 Thessalonians 5:19 (KJV)

Where the Spirit is welcomed and evangelism is prioritized, the fire returns. The church begins to burn again—not with gimmicks, but with glory.

CHAPTER 4

REIGNITING PASSION IN THE PULPIT AND THE PEW

> "Is not my word like as a fire? saith the Lord; and like a hammer that breaketh the rock in pieces?" —Jeremiah 23:29 (KJV)

The fire of soul winning does not begin with programs—it begins with passion. And that passion must be reignited both in the pulpit and in the pew. When leaders burn for the lost, the people will follow. When the congregation embraces the burden, the church becomes unstoppable.

The Pulpit Must Burn Again

Many pulpits today are polished but powerless. They inspire, educate, and entertain—but they do not ignite. The early church had no microphones, lights, or media, but their messages shook cities and brought people to repentance. Why? Because their hearts burned with holy fire.

> "Then I said, I will not make mention of him, nor speak any more in his name. But his word was in mine heart as a burning fire shut up in my bones…" —Jeremiah 20:9 (KJV)

Reigniting the Fire of Soul Winning in Our Churches

The fire must return to our sermons. Not just clever outlines, but convicting truth. Not just church growth strategies, but soul salvation urgency. When preachers stop preaching for response and start preaching for repentance, the fire will return.

How the Pulpit Can Reignite

The pulpit is not just a platform—it is a prophetic launching pad. What burns in the pulpit will set fire to the pews. What is ignored in the pulpit will be absent in the people. If soul winning is not modeled and emphasized from the top, it will be marginalized throughout the church.

If the church is going to reignite its fire for evangelism, it must begin with the shepherds, the preachers, and the pulpits that shape culture, doctrine, and spiritual direction. There are four practical and prophetic ways the pulpit can lead the church back to the harvest.

1. **Preach Repentance, Sin, Hell, and Heaven with Truth and Love**

The modern pulpit has become increasingly uncomfortable with topics like sin, repentance, hell, and judgment. But these are not just doctrines—they are foundations of the gospel. A church that no longer preaches repentance cannot produce true conversion.

A pulpit on fire will:

- Call sin what it is, without shame or compromise.
- Preach repentance not as a punishment, but as a pathway to life.

- Remind the church that hell is real, but so is grace.
- Proclaim heaven as our hope, and Christ as the only door.

This isn't about harshness—it's about truth wrapped in love. Jesus preached about hell with tears in His eyes. John the Baptist cried out "Repent!" to prepare people for Jesus.

The church won't run toward the cross if we don't tell them what they're being saved from.

2. Testify Regularly About Soul-Winning Experiences and Salvations

The pulpit should not only preach the Word, it should testify to what the Word is producing in real life.

When pastors and leaders share:

- Personal encounters in witnessing
- Testimonies of salvations
- Moments where the gospel pierced a heart
- Stories of lives transformed through outreach

…it ignites faith in the hearts of the congregation. It models that evangelism is not a department—it's a daily lifestyle.

Testimony releases three things:

- **Encouragement:** "If God used them, He can use me."
- **Expectation:** "This isn't just doctrine—it's happening now."

Reigniting the Fire of Soul Winning in Our Churches

- **Impartation:** "That same fire can fall on me."

Don't just teach soul winning—celebrate it. Speak it. Multiply it.

3. Prioritize Altar Calls and Gospel Invitations

A fireless pulpit may preach well, but it doesn't call for a decision. Sermons may end in applause or transition, but not in conviction and surrender. That must change.

Every time the gospel is preached, the listener should be:

- Confronted with truth.
- Invited to repentance.
- Offered new life through Christ.

If you preach the gospel and don't give people an opportunity to respond, it's like lighting a match but refusing to offer the flame.

A church that prioritizes altar calls:

- Makes room for the Holy Spirit.
- Keeps the focus on eternity.
- Trains believers to bring guests in faith.
- Sees the altar as a delivery room, not a closing moment.

Don't let the altar be forgotten. That's where chains break. That's where the lost come home. That's where the fire spreads.

4. Train the Church From the Pulpit to See Evangelism as a Lifestyle

The pulpit is not just for inspiration—it's for impartation and equipping. Soul winning should not be reduced to events and outreach programs. It must be preached as a lifestyle that every believer carries.

How to train from the pulpit:

- Preach messages that teach how to witness.
- Model conversational evangelism.
- Celebrate members who lead others to Christ.
- Equip saints to evangelize in their schools, jobs, and neighborhoods.
- Tie evangelism into spiritual maturity, not just church growth.

Declare it often: *"You are a soul winner. This gospel is not just for you—it's flowing through you."*

Let the pulpit become a place where:

- Disciples are trained.
- Fear is broken.
- Boldness is imparted.
- Evangelism is normalized.

When the Pulpit Burns, the Church Follows

The fire must start in the pulpit.
If we want soul-winning churches, we need soul-winning leaders.
If we want revival, we must call for repentance.
If we want souls, we must make room at the altar.

Reigniting the Fire of Soul Winning in Our Churches

— Preach the cross.
— Preach the blood.
— Preach with urgency.
— Preach for transformation.

Let the pulpit burn again, because where the pulpit leads, the church follows.

The Pew Must Carry the Fire Too

The church is not a stage and an audience—it is a body. If only the pastor is on fire, the building might be warm. But when the people burn, the city feels the heat.

> **"And they were all filled with the Holy Ghost, and began to speak…" —Acts 2:4 (KJV)**

The fire of Pentecost didn't just fill the apostles—it filled everyone in the upper room, and everyone of them became a witness. The pew must carry this same boldness today.

Signs of fire in the pew:

- Members share their faith without prompting.
- Salvations happen outside the sanctuary.
- Believers pray for the lost by name.
- The atmosphere is evangelistic, not just emotional.

Practical ways to reignite passion:

1. **Testimonies:** Let people share recent soul winning encounters during services.

2. **Training:** Host evangelism workshops and encourage one-on-one witnessing.

3. **Outreach Challenges:** Issue monthly challenges to reach new people with the gospel.

4. **Leadership Modeling:** If pastors and leaders are going out, the people will too.

Let Fire Flow from Pulpit to Pew

When both leaders and members are gripped by the urgency of the gospel, the church becomes a living flame. The community won't just hear sermons—they'll see the Savior in the streets.

> **"…the Lord working with them, and confirming the word with signs following." —Mark 16:20 (KJV)**

CHAPTER 5

RESTORING EVANGELISM TO THE CORE OF CHURCH CULTURE

> "And daily in the temple, and in every house, they ceased not to teach and preach Jesus Christ." —Acts 5:42 (KJV)

In many churches today, evangelism has become a category rather than a culture. It's something scheduled rather than something shared. The early church didn't relegate outreach to a calendar slot—it was woven into their DNA.

If the fire of soul winning is to be reignited, evangelism must move from the periphery to the core of church culture.

Culture Is More Powerful Than Programming

Programs may inspire for a moment. Culture transforms for a lifetime. You can run an outreach event—but that won't change the culture unless the people are discipled into a mindset of mission.

> "Go ye therefore, and teach all nations... Teaching them to observe all things..." —Matthew 28:19–20 (KJV)

Jesus didn't just commission them to make converts—He told them to build a culture of obedience. That includes obeying the call to reach others.

What Does a Soul Winning Church Culture Look Like?

A church may have great preaching, powerful music, and beautiful buildings, but if it lacks a culture of soul winning, it has missed its mission. The true measure of a Spirit-filled church is not just how many gather but how many are being transformed and sent.

Soul winning is not an event.
It's not a quarterly outreach.
It's a culture—a way of life rooted in the heart of the church.

A soul-winning church breathes evangelism in every room, every service, every conversation. Here's what that culture looks like in action:

1. Evangelism Is Talked About Weekly

In a soul-winning church, evangelism is not a footnote—it's front and center. It's in the sermons. It's in the testimonies. It's in the announcements and the small groups. Why? Because leaders talk about what they love. And when the leadership burns for souls, the people catch fire.

You'll hear things like:

- "Who did you share Jesus with this week?"
- "Let's pray for our unsaved family members right now."
- "This Sunday, bring someone who needs Christ."

Evangelism is not just encouraged—it's expected, celebrated, and woven into the identity of the church.

2. New Believers Are Being Added Regularly

A soul-winning culture produces new spiritual births consistently. Church growth is not just measured in attendance, but in transformation.

You know the difference:

- **Transfer growth:** Christians moving from one church to another.
- **Conversion growth:** Sinners becoming saints through repentance and faith in Christ.

In a soul-winning church:

- The lost feel welcome to come.
- The Word is preached with clarity.
- Altar calls are consistently given.
- Discipleship begins the moment someone says "yes" to Jesus.

It's not about the numbers—it's about new names written in the Lamb's Book of Life.

3. The Lost Are Welcomed and Pursued

Soul-winning churches are not just warm—they are intentional.

There's a difference between being friendly to the lost and pursuing the lost.

Reigniting the Fire of Soul Winning in Our Churches

In this kind of culture:

- Members see themselves as missionaries.
- Visitors are greeted with genuine love and follow-up.
- Sermons are spiritually rich yet accessible to the unchurched.
- The atmosphere is holy, but not intimidating.

Evangelism isn't just about what happens in the street—it's about how the lost are treated when they walk through your doors.

You can tell a soul-winning church by how it welcomes broken people.

4. Outreach Is a Natural Part of Conversation

In soul-winning churches, outreach isn't awkward or forced—it's a normal part of life. People talk about it like they do birthdays or sports.

You'll hear:

- "Who are you praying for this week?"
- "Let's go witness together this weekend."
- "Hey, I brought my coworker to church—can we pray over them?"

It's not religious hype—it's a genuine burden for souls that spills into everyday speech. Conversations aren't just surface level—they're Spirit-led.

Evangelism becomes:

- The language of the lobby.
- The rhythm of prayer groups.
- The topic in team meetings.

Where evangelism is spoken often, it is acted on boldly.

5. Baptism Becomes a Regular Celebration

Baptism is not just a ceremony—it's a supernatural testimony that people are crossing from death to life. In soul-winning churches, baptism is frequent, joyful, and highly prioritized.

It is evidence that:

- The gospel is being preached.
- People are responding.
- Discipleship is happening.
- Heaven is rejoicing.

Baptism Sundays in these churches are:

- Joyful, with loud celebration.
- Powerful, with public confession.
- Evangelistic, with friends and families watching lives be changed.

Some churches baptize monthly, others weekly—but in a soul-winning church, it's expected that people will be baptized regularly because salvation is happening regularly.

Soul-Winning Culture Doesn't Happen by Accident

You can program a service. You can plan an event. But you cannot fake a culture.

A soul-winning culture must be:

- Modeled by leaders.
- Preached from the pulpit.
- Prayed over by intercessors.
- Activated by every believer.

It's time for the church to go beyond church growth strategies and return to kingdom expansion through soul winning.

Beyond Church Growth–Back to Kingdom Expansion

We live in a generation that has mastered the mechanics of church growth but forgotten the mandate of kingdom expansion. We've strategized, optimized, branded, and built—but far too often, we've done so without burden for the lost.

It's time to return. Not to bigger buildings or better lighting—but to the basics of the gospel:

- The blood.
- The cross.
- The call to repent.
- The mission to reach.
- The cry of heaven: "Who will go?"

Church growth fills seats.
Kingdom expansion saves souls.
Church growth can happen through transfer.
Kingdom expansion happens through transformation.

1. Let the Culture Be Birthed

A soul-winning culture isn't manufactured. It's birthed in prayer and sustained through obedience.

It begins when:

- Leaders are broken again over the harvest.
- Members begin to pray by name for the lost.
- Evangelism becomes a normal expectation, not an optional event.
- Every ministry in the church is filtered through this question: *"Does this help reach or disciple souls?"*

When that becomes the mindset, culture is no longer something you implement—it's something you carry.

This culture is Spirit-born. It's altar-driven. And it's always burning with eternal urgency.

2. Let the Fire Spread

The fire of soul winning is contagious. Once it touches one heart, it begins to move through a church, a city, a region.

- One soul on fire becomes a family transformed.

Reigniting the Fire of Soul Winning in Our Churches

- One outreach leads to an entire block hearing the gospel.
- One testimony brings 10 more to the altar.
- One youth group revival changes a school.

The fire spreads when:

- Leaders preach with urgency.
- Intercessors pray with travail.
- Believers go with boldness.
- The Holy Spirit is welcomed without restriction.

Let the fire spread—until it's impossible to attend your church without encountering the living Christ.

3. Let the Altars Overflow

In a soul-winning church, the altar is the center of everything.

— It's not rushed.
— It's not skipped.
— It's not ignored.

The altar becomes:

- A place of repentance.
- A place of tears.
- A place of miracles.
- A place where sinners are reborn and saints are reignited.

Overflowing altars are evidence of a church that is alive—not with hype, but with holy fire.

Pastor Dr. Claudine Benjamin

Let the altar be full again—not of noise, but of brokenness.

A cold altar leads to cold hearts.

A burning altar leads to a burning house of revival.

4. Let the Lost Come Home

Jesus died for people—not programs, platforms, or performances. The church exists to call prodigals home.

In a soul-winning culture:

- The lost feel loved without being entertained.
- The broken feel welcomed without compromise.
- The gospel is clear, not diluted.
- Grace is powerful, not passive.
- The message is consistent: "Come home."

Every song, sermon, service should extend the heart of the Father to the one who's wandered: *"We've been expecting you. The robe is ready. The ring is waiting. The feast has been prepared."*

Let the lost come home.

And let the church be the house that runs to meet them.

5. This Is What a Soul-Winning Church Looks Like

It's not defined by:

Reigniting the Fire of Soul Winning in Our Churches

- The size of the sanctuary.
- The smoothness of transitions.
- The volume of the music.
- The number of followers on social media.

It's defined by:

- Burdened hearts.
- Bold proclamation.
- Burning altars.
- Baptism celebrations.
- Brokenness in worship.
- A constant stream of souls being born again

This is what the early church looked like.
This is what Jesus died to establish.
And this is what the world desperately needs today.

Let It Begin in Us

We declare:

- Let the culture be birthed.
- Let the fire spread.
- Let the altars overflow.
- Let the lost come home.

Let the church burn again with the fire of soul winning.
Because a church on fire cannot be ignored.
A church on fire cannot be silent.

A church on fire will shake the city, shift the region, and populate heaven.
This is more than revival.
This is rescue.

Lord, reignite us.
Until the harvest is gathered.
Until heaven rejoices.
Until You return.

Shift Every Ministry to Support the Mission

- Youth ministries must teach teens to reach their peers.

- Men's and women's ministries should include evangelistic fellowship.

- Choirs and worship teams should remember that their song prepares hearts to receive the gospel.

- Hospitality teams should welcome guests as potential disciples, not just visitors.

"Let all things be done unto edifying." —1 Corinthians 14:26 (KJV)

Every part of the church should lead toward the harvest.

Practical Ways to Restore Evangelism to the Culture

1. **Vision Casting:** Preach a series on evangelism and the urgency of the great commission.

2. **Celebrate Wins:** Highlight new salvations in every service. Create joy around outreach.

3. **Integrate Evangelism Training:** Make it part of membership classes and leadership onboarding.

4. **Create Space for the Lost:** Plan services with seekers in mind. Use clear gospel invitations.

From Occasional to Foundational

When evangelism is restored to the core of the church, everything else becomes more fruitful. Discipleship is deeper. Prayer becomes focused. Worship becomes intimate—because nothing fuels the church like seeing souls saved.

> **"Likewise, I say unto you, there is joy in the presence of the angels of God over one sinner that repenteth." —Luke 15:10 (KJV)**

The fire doesn't come from attendance—it comes from harvest.

Creating a Culture of Compassion-Driven Outreach

> **"But when he saw the multitudes, he was moved with compassion on them…" —Matthew 9:36a (KJV)**

True evangelism isn't driven by duty—it's driven by compassion. Programs may produce activity, but only compassion produces impact. Without compassion, outreach becomes a chore. With compassion, it becomes a mission fueled by love.

If we are to reignite the fire of soul winning, we must build a church culture where compassion leads to action.

Jesus Was Moved by Compassion—Not Strategy

Jesus didn't launch a 12-month evangelism campaign. He didn't form committees to analyze outreach methods. He saw the need, and He was moved.

> **"And Jesus, moved with compassion, put forth his hand..."**
> **—Mark 1:41a (KJV)**

Compassion isn't a feeling—it's a force. It pushes you out of comfort and into service. It's the bridge between observation and obedience.

The Church Must Feel Again

One of the greatest dangers of modern Christianity is emotional numbness. We've seen so much pain that we've become desensitized. But you cannot rescue what you no longer notice.

> **"Mine eye affecteth mine heart..." —Lamentations 3:51a (KJV)**

What you consistently expose your eyes to will eventually shape the condition of your heart. A church that avoids the broken, addicted, and unsaved will soon lose its ability to feel what God feels.

Signs of a compassion-driven church:

1. People cry out for the lost in prayer—not just their personal needs.

2. Outreach is not occasional—it's ongoing.

3. Evangelism is talked about not just from the pulpit, but in the pews.

4. The hurting are welcomed, not judged.

5. Testimonies of transformation are celebrated regularly.

Compassion Must Be Discipled

Compassion is not just caught—it must be taught.

> **"Bear ye one another's burdens, and so fulfil the law of Christ." —Galatians 6:2 (KJV)**

That means:

- Leaders must model it.
- Discipleship programs must include it.
- Church events must reflect it.
- Conversations must stir it.

Let people serve in places where they will see needs—homeless shelters, prisons, hospitals, and streets. Exposure to pain awakens purpose.

Compassion Must Become the Why Behind the What

When compassion becomes the reason we evangelize, the church becomes unstoppable. Outreach isn't something we have to do—it's something we can't help but do.

> **"For the love of Christ constraineth us…" —2 Corinthians 5:14a (KJV)**

Only love can sustain long-term soul winning. Guilt may start the work, but only compassion will keep it burning.

CHAPTER 6

EQUIPPING THE SAINTS – TURNING BELIEVERS INTO BOLD WITNESSES

> "And he gave some… evangelists… for the perfecting of the saints, for the work of the ministry…" —Ephesians 4:11–12 (KJV)

The purpose of ministry leadership is not to entertain or impress, but to equip. God's design is for every believer—not just pastors or evangelists—to be trained for the work of the kingdom. This includes bold, everyday witnessing.

Churches that burn with evangelism are churches that equip the saints to be soul winners.

Why Many Believers Don't Witness

It's not usually rebellion—it's lack of training.

Many believers genuinely love God, attend church faithfully, and desire to be used—but never share their faith. Why?

It's not usually rebellion or cold-heartedness.
It's lack of preparation.
It's fear.
It's misunderstanding.
It's intimidation.

Reigniting the Fire of Soul Winning in Our Churches

The enemy has deceived many Christians into silence by convincing them they're unqualified, unequipped, or unworthy to evangelize. As a result, too many churches are filled with passionate worshipers who never witness, and committed disciples who never disciple.

They Don't Know What to Say

Most Christians aren't silent because they don't care—they're silent because they're unsure how to speak.

Common thoughts:

- "What if I say it wrong?"
- "What if they ask questions I can't answer?"
- "What if I mess up someone's view of God?"

This reveals a training gap. If we don't teach people how to clearly and simply present the gospel, we leave them paralyzed in uncertainty.

Solution:

- Teach believers a basic 3-minute gospel outline (God loves, sin separates, Jesus saves, you must respond).
- Equip them to share their testimony in 60 seconds.
- Provide gospel tracts or cards with key scriptures and follow-up steps.

Evangelism is not about eloquence—it's about obedience.

The Holy Spirit empowers what you speak, not how polished you sound.

They Fear Rejection or Feeling Unprepared

Fear is one of the greatest barriers to soul winning. It's the quiet killer of boldness and compassion.

Believers fear:

- Being laughed at.
- Being ignored.
- Being labeled "weird" or "religious."
- Not having the answers

But Jesus never promised comfort—He promised companionship in the mission.

Fear shrinks when confidence grows. Confidence grows through:

- Practice.
- Community support.
- Testimonies of obedience.
- The empowering of the Holy Spirit.

Encourage your church: Rejection of the message isn't rejection of the messenger. You're planting seeds—even if you don't see the harvest.

Reigniting the Fire of Soul Winning in Our Churches

They Believe It's the Pastor's Job

Many believers think evangelism is a title-based task. They've been conditioned to believe it belongs to:

- Pastors
- Evangelists
- Outreach directors
- Special event speakers

This is a cultural error, and it has weakened the church.

The truth is: Evangelism is not for the elite—it's for the obedient.

The great commission was given to the whole church, not just a few leaders. Every believer is a carrier of the gospel.

Every neighborhood, workplace, classroom, and city needs more than one preacher—it needs a mobilized people.

Churches must teach members:

- You don't need a mic to minister.
- You don't need a license to be a light.
- You don't need a title to lead someone to Jesus.

They've Never Been Taught How to Share Their Faith

This may be the most honest reason—and the most solvable.

    — You can't do what you haven't been taught.
    — You can't model what you haven't seen.

— You can't live what hasn't been preached to you.

Many churches have rich teaching on spiritual growth, family, giving, and prayer, but never train believers in personal evangelism.

It's time to fix that.

Churches must:

- Create workshops and small groups around evangelism.
- Model witnessing from the pulpit and in testimonies.
- Equip every ministry team to be ready to lead someone to Jesus.
- Normalize evangelism in every age group—from kids to seniors

When believers are taught, trained, and activated—they become bold.

Equip the Saints—Ignite the Harvest

We cannot expect soul-winning results without soul-winning instruction.

The church must not only pray for revival—but prepare for it.

If we want a soul-winning church, we must become a soul-equipping church.

— Let the laborers rise.
— Let the fear break.

Reigniting the Fire of Soul Winning in Our Churches

— Let the equipping begin.
— Let the silence end.

Because every believer is a voice—and every soul is worth it.

Training Transforms Fear Into Boldness

"The wicked flee when no man pursueth: but the righteous are bold as a lion." —Proverbs 28:1 (KJV)

Boldness doesn't come from personality—it comes from preparation and power.

Equip your church by teaching:

- The basic gospel message (Creation → Fall → Redemption → Response).
- How to share personal testimony.
- How to lead someone in a salvation prayer.
- How to answer common objections.
- How to recognize divine appointments.

Make Evangelism Training a Priority

Don't hide it in a side room once a quarter. Make it central to your church's rhythm.

Ways to train:

- Monthly soul winning classes.
- Role-play exercises during small groups.
- Commission outreach leaders to disciple others.
- Provide printable or digital gospel tracts.

- Teach youth and children how to share their faith too.

"A man that is an heretick after the first and second admonition reject…" —Titus 3:10 (KJV)

Even correcting false doctrine requires a foundation in truth—and believers must be equipped to defend and proclaim the gospel.

Equip, Empower, and Expect Fruit

Equip your people. Empower them through encouragement and opportunity. Then expect the harvest. As they grow in skill and confidence, they will step out boldly.

"But sanctify the Lord God in your hearts: and be ready always to give an answer to every man that asketh you…" —1 Peter 3:15a (KJV)

When believers are equipped, they don't wait for church events—they live on mission every day.

CHAPTER 7

CREATING A CULTURE OF COMPASSIONATE-DRIVEN OUTREACH

> "This is my commandment, That ye love one another, as I have loved you." —John 15:12 (KJV)

Churches that win souls consistently do so not because of trendy programs or talented teams, but because they cultivate a culture of compassion. Compassion-driven outreach isn't rooted in obligation or formality. It flows from a church that feels deeply and acts accordingly.

Outreach is not merely an event on the calendar—it's a reflection of the heartbeat of the people.

From Projects to Lifestyle

A church may host outreach events occasionally, but a church that has built a culture of outreach lives it daily. It's in their language, **prayers, stories, udget, and planning.**

> "Let all your things be done with charity." —1 Corinthians 16:14 (KJV)

Churches must transition from sporadic events to consistent acts of love that respond to real community needs, for example:

- Food drives.
- Prison and hospital visits.
- Community service.
- Street evangelism.
- Intentional connection with newcomers and the unchurched.

What Compassionate Outreach Looks Like

1. **Presence before preaching** – Show up where people are hurting before handing them a tract.

2. **Listening before leading** – Listen to stories. Pain often opens hearts to truth.

3. **Consistency over convenience** – Outreach can't be seasonal; compassion is ongoing.

4. **Dignity with the message** – The gospel must be delivered with humility and respect.

"And of some have compassion, making a difference." — Jude 1:22 (KJV)

Compassion opens the door to conversation. When the church builds trust in the community, it earns the right to speak truth.

Compassion Must Touch Every Ministry

- Ushers and greeters should treat every person as if they matter eternally.

- Worship teams must prepare the atmosphere with hearts focused on the lost.

- Small group leaders should regularly challenge members to reach others.

- Children's ministries must teach the next generation to see others through the eyes of Jesus.

When every team and every member carries the burden for souls, outreach becomes more than an event—it becomes who we are.

CHAPTER 8

OVERCOMING FEAR, APATHY, AND DISTRACTION IN EVANGELISM

> **"For God hath not given us the spirit of fear; but of power, and of love, and of a sound mind."** —2 Timothy 1:7 (KJV)

The greatest barriers to soul winning are not external—they are internal. They exist in the hearts and minds of believers:

- **Fear:** "What if I say the wrong thing?"
- **Apathy:** "Someone else will reach them."
- **Distraction:** "I'm too busy right now."

These enemies silently kill passion for the lost. They must be named, confronted, and overcome.

Fear Must Be Replaced with Faith

Many Christians avoid witnessing because they fear rejection, confrontation, or failure. But the power to overcome fear is already within us.

> **"…ye shall receive power, after that the Holy Ghost is come upon you: and ye shall be witnesses…"** —Acts 1:8 (KJV)

Fear is a spirit—but so is boldness. You overcome fear not by waiting until you feel brave, but by stepping out in faith.

Strategies for overcoming fear:

- Practice sharing your story in a safe setting (small groups, friends).

- Memorize a simple gospel presentation.

- Pray for boldness daily and act on small promptings.

Apathy Must Be Replaced with Urgency

Apathy is not hatred—it's indifference. It says, *"I'm glad I'm saved"* and forgets about those who aren't. This is one of the most dangerous conditions in the church today.

> **"Lift up your eyes, and look on the fields; for they are white already to harvest." —John 4:35b (KJV)**

Jesus told His disciples to look again. Sometimes the harvest is lost not because it isn't ready, but because the church is asleep.

How to overcome apathy:

- Fast for a renewed burden.

- Volunteer in places where pain is visible (hospitals, shelters, prisons).

- Read books and testimonies about salvation and missionary work.

- Meditate on the reality of eternity.

Distraction Must Be Replaced with Discipline

Life is loud. We are often too busy to notice divine opportunities. But soul winners aren't people with more time—they are people with more focus.

> **"Walk in wisdom toward them that are without, redeeming the time." —Colossians 4:5 (KJV)**

To overcome distraction:

- Schedule time to intentionally reach out.

- Turn off noise (social media, entertainment) and ask God for divine appointments.

- Slow down. The Holy Spirit speaks most clearly in stillness.

The Internal Shift Must Begin in the Church

Fear, apathy, and distraction are not just personal but cultural. Church leaders must address these enemies from the pulpit, from the classroom, and in conversation.

The church cannot afford to wait until people feel ready. We must teach them to move in obedience, not just emotion.

CHAPTER 9

THE ROLE OF LEADERSHIP IN MODELING THE MISSION

"Be ye followers of me, even as I also am of Christ." —1 Corinthians 11:1 (KJV)

The culture of a church is shaped more by what is modeled than by what is taught. Leaders set the tone. If pastors and ministry heads do not live the mission, the congregation will not prioritize it either. Leadership must do more than support soul winning—they must embody it.

Pastors Must Lead by Example

Preaching evangelism is not enough. People must see their pastors witnessing in the community, praying for the lost, and celebrating conversions.

"How shall they preach, except they be sent?" —Romans 10:15a (KJV)

Pastors are not just proclaimers—they are mobilizers. Their example either builds or breaks the evangelistic culture.

Ways pastors can model the mission:

- Share personal soul winning stories.
- Participate in outreach events—not just endorse them.

Reigniting the Fire of Soul Winning in Our Churches

- Keep the gospel central in every message.
- Lead altar calls with urgency and clarity.

Ministry Leaders Must Make Evangelism a Priority

Every department head must infuse their area with the mission. Evangelism is not just for outreach coordinators—it belongs in:

- Worship rehearsals.
- Usher meetings.
- Youth planning sessions.
- Choir devotionals.

"Whatever you do, do it all for the glory of God." —1 Corinthians 10:31 (paraphrased)

The glory of God is magnified when the lost are brought home.

Train the Next Generation by Example

The leaders of tomorrow are watching the leaders of today. Young people are hungry for purpose, but if we model programs over passion, they will inherit structure without fire.

Let them witness boldness. Let them be trained by the flame, not just the format.

Honor What You Want to Multiply

If you want soul winning to increase, you must celebrate it. Celebrate every salvation. Every testimony. Every step of obedience.

What gets honored gets repeated.

> **"And let us consider one another to provoke unto love and to good works."** —Hebrews 10:24 (KJV)

Leaders must provoke their people—not to performance, but to fruitfulness.

CHAPTER 10

PRACTICAL STRATEGIES TO REIGNITE EVANGELISM IN YOUR CHURCH

"And the Lord said unto the servant, Go out into the highways and hedges, and compel them to come in, that my house may be filled." —Luke 14:23 (KJV)

A passion for evangelism must be matched with a plan. While the fire for soul winning begins in the heart, it flourishes through intentional action. Churches that reignite evangelism do not simply talk about outreach—they build systems, structures, and schedules that make outreach inevitable.

This chapter focuses on practical, scalable strategies your church can implement to move from inspiration to impact.

1. Preach an evangelism series annually.

If your people never hear about the harvest, they'll assume it isn't urgent. A once-a-year preaching series on evangelism:

- Rekindles urgency.
- Refocuses the church on the mission.
- Equips new members with a biblical foundation.

Reigniting the Fire of Soul Winning in Our Churches

Include messages on:

- The great commission (see Matthew 28:19–20).
- The urgency of the harvest (see John 4:35).
- The role of every believer (see 2 Corinthians 5:18–20).

2. Launch a weekly evangelism training track.

Create an ongoing, rotating course that equips believers to:

- Share the gospel clearly (see Romans 10:9–10).
- Use their testimony as a tool (see Revelation 12:11).
- Overcome fear and rejection (see Proverbs 28:1).
- Pray effectively for the lost (1 Timothy 2:1–4).

Make this part of your church's growth pathway—not just an optional event.

3. Mobilize every ministry.

Embed soul winning goals into the fabric of every ministry:

- Children's church teaches how to pray for unsaved parents.
- Youth group has a "bring a friend" night monthly.
- Men's and women's groups take turns doing monthly outreach.
- Worship teams pray for salvation impact during services.

"Let every one of us please his neighbour for his good to edification." —Romans 15:2 (KJV)

Every ministry must ask, *"How are we reaching those who don't yet know Christ?"*

4. Host "Compel Sundays"

Choose one Sunday per quarter to focus entirely on reaching the lost. Challenge members to bring someone who needs Jesus. Make everything—from worship to preaching—gospel-focused and clear.

> **"And he said unto them, Go ye into all the world, and preach the gospel to every creature." —Mark 16:15 (KJV)**

Follow up with prayer, personal connections, and discipleship pathways for those who respond.

5. Provide easy evangelism tools.

Equip members with:

- Printed and digital gospel tracts.
- "Invite cards" for services.
- Social media graphics they can share.
- Testimony cards and salvation follow-up guides.

Make it easy to reach out by giving them the right tools, then train them how to use them.

6. Measure and celebrate soul winning fruit.

What gets celebrated gets repeated.

Track:

- First-time decisions for Christ.
- Baptisms.
- Outreach participation.

- Personal testimonies.

Recognize and honor those stepping out. Not to glorify man, but to provoke the church into greater works.

> **"Let your light so shine before men, that they may see your good works, and glorify your Father..." —Matthew 5:16 (KJV)**

CHAPTER 11

RAISING UP A NEW GENERATION OF SOUL WINNERS

> "One generation shall praise thy works to another, and shall declare thy mighty acts." —Psalm 145:4 (KJV)

The future of evangelism is not in a program—it's in a person. The fire of soul winning must be passed down to the next generation, or it will flicker out when the current generation finishes its race. Young people are not just the church of tomorrow—they are soul winners today.

This chapter is about how to raise up a generation that burns with the gospel.

1. Teach evangelism early and often.

Don't wait until teens are 18 to introduce them to outreach. Children can be taught:

- What it means to be saved.
- How to pray for others.
- How to invite friends to church.
- How to be light in dark places.

> "Train up a child in the way he should go…" —Proverbs 22:6a (KJV)

Reigniting the Fire of Soul Winning in Our Churches

Include evangelism in Sunday school lessons, youth devotionals, and even Vacation Bible School themes.

2. Make evangelism practical for youth.

Today's teens are hungry for real purpose. Equip them with:

- Short gospel presentations for peers.
- Real-life role-playing and Q&A sessions.
- "Bring-a-friend" challenges tied to incentives and testimonies.

Provide mission experiences—neighborhood canvassing, outreach in parks, and local service projects—so they develop courage in real-world settings.

> **"Let no man despise thy youth; but be thou an example of the believers…" —1 Timothy 4:12 (KJV)**

3. Model it in leadership.

Young people will not do what you say—they will do what you live. Youth leaders, children's ministry workers, and mentors must be active soul winners.

Let the next generation see their leaders:

- Praying for the lost by name.
- Reaching out to neighbors and classmates.
- Leading someone to Christ one-on-one.

Discipleship happens by example.

4. Share stories of revival and soul winning impact.

Young people are deeply inspired by testimonies of transformation.

Show them:

- Video testimonies of teenagers getting saved and changed.
- Stories of missionaries who risked everything.
- Real-time accounts of how the gospel is working today.

This creates holy curiosity and fuels their desire to be part of something bigger than themselves.

> **"And they overcame him by the blood of the Lamb, and by the word of their testimony..." —Revelation 12:11 (KJV)**

5. Empower and release them.

Don't keep youth in the background. **Let them:**

- Serve on outreach teams.
- Lead evangelistic moments during services.
- Create outreach-focused content on social media.
- Pray and fast for revival in their schools.

Equip them, yes—but also trust them. They will rise to the level of your expectation.

> **"...your sons and your daughters shall prophesy..." —Joel 2:28 (KJV)**

CHAPTER 12

STAYING ON FIRE – KEEPING EVANGELISM AT THE HEART

> "Wherefore I put thee in remembrance that thou stir up the gift of God, which is in thee…" —2 Timothy 1:6 (KJV)

It's one thing to ignite the fire of soul winning—it's another to keep it burning. Many churches begin with a burst of evangelistic momentum, only to fizzle out after the excitement fades. But sustainable evangelism isn't emotional—it's intentional.

A church that stays on fire must continually return to the source of the fire: the Holy Spirit, the Word of God, and the burden for lost souls.

1. **Revisit the vision regularly.**

Leaders must cast the evangelistic vision often. Don't assume people remember. **Remind them:**

- Why we reach out (see Luke 19:10).
- What's at stake (see Romans 6:23).
- What God expects (see Matthew 28:19–20).

Keep the mission before them until it becomes part of them.

2. **Create a system of evangelism accountability.**

Reigniting the Fire of Soul Winning in Our Churches

You don't drift into soul winning. You choose it.

Establish accountability systems like:

- Monthly reports of salvations and contacts made.
- Teams that meet to strategize and pray.
- Personal evangelism goals for members and leaders.

"So then every one of us shall give account of himself to God." —Romans 14:12 (KJV)

When people know they'll be asked about their outreach efforts, they're more likely to stay focused.

3. Keep evangelism in prayer and fasting.

You can't maintain spiritual fire in the flesh. Prayer and fasting help keep evangelism Spirit-empowered rather than effort-driven.

Host monthly prayer nights focused entirely on:

- The lost in your city.
- Boldness for your people.
- Specific souls you're pursuing.

"The effectual fervent prayer of a righteous man availeth much." —James 5:16b (KJV)

4. Keep the fire fresh with testimonies.

When people see that evangelism is working, it fuels them to keep going.

— Share testimonies weekly.
— Invite new converts to speak.

— Show video highlights of recent outreach results.

Let the church hear the stories until the stories become part of the culture.

5. Keep evangelism on the calendar.

If evangelism doesn't make it to the calendar, it won't last.

— Plan quarterly outreach Sundays.
— Schedule monthly evangelism training.
— Rotate ministry teams into outreach opportunities.

Structure sustains fire. Fire without a plan will eventually burn out.

"Not slothful in business; fervent in spirit; serving the Lord;" —Romans 12:11 (KJV)

CHAPTER 13

PROFILES OF IMPACT – CHARACTERS OF SOUL WINNING FIRE

Evangelism didn't start with us, and it won't end with us. Scripture and history give us powerful examples of people who carried the soul winning fire, inspiring us to do the same. Their lives reveal what kind of character fuels a church's mission.

1. **Jesus Christ – The Original Evangelist**

"For the Son of man is come to seek and to save that which was lost." —Luke 19:10 (KJV)

Jesus didn't just teach about evangelism—He lived it. He sought out individuals one by one.

He modeled truth wrapped in compassion and pursuit wrapped in patience. Every soul mattered.

Zacchaeus in the Tree – Evangelism That Sees the Overlooked

"And when Jesus came to the place, he looked up, and saw him…" —Luke 19:5 (KJV)

Zacchaeus was a wealthy tax collector—a man despised by his own people. He was powerful, yet empty. Outwardly successful, yet spiritually bankrupt. Most of the crowd saw a sinner. Jesus saw a soul.

Jesus could have passed by. He could have ignored Zacchaeus like everyone else did. But He looked up—and called him down by name.

Evangelism Begins With Vision

Jesus saw what others missed:

- A seeker hiding in shame.
- A man longing for more.
- A sinner ready for salvation.

Evangelism Begins With Vision

"But when he saw the multitudes, he was moved with compassion on them…"—Matthew 9:36 (KJV)

Evangelism doesn't start with a microphone. It doesn't begin on a stage. It doesn't even begin with a sermon.

Evangelism begins with vision—the ability to see people not as they appear, but as they truly are: souls made in God's image, living under the weight of sin, and desperately in need of redemption.

This is why many churches struggle to evangelize—not because they lack programs, but because they lack sight.

A church that can't see the harvest won't reach for it.

Jesus Saw What Others Missed

Throughout His ministry, Jesus consistently saw beyond appearances and perceived the heart. Where others saw a reputation, a label, or an inconvenience, Jesus saw:

- A divine appointment.
- A soul on the edge of eternity.
- A person worth pursuing.

Let's look at three key encounters that reveal how evangelism flows from God-given vision.

1. **He saw a seeker hiding in shame — The Woman at the Well**

"Then cometh a woman of Samaria to draw water: Jesus saith unto her, Give me to drink." —John 4:7 (KJV)

No one else saw her value. She came to the well at noon to avoid the crowd. Her past was broken. Her heart was ashamed. But Jesus saw past her scandal and into her spirit.

He didn't see:

- A problem to avoid.
- A sinner to condemn.
- A woman to expose.

He saw:

- A soul thirsty for truth.
- A worshiper buried beneath shame.
- An evangelist in the making.

Because Jesus saw her rightly, He reached her personally, and she won her whole city.

Application

Evangelism begins when we see past people's sin, skin, and status and recognize their need for living water.

2. He saw a man longing for more — Zacchaeus in the Tree

"And when Jesus came to the place, he looked up, and saw him…" —Luke 19:5 (KJV)

Others saw Zacchaeus as a corrupt tax collector. But Jesus saw a man climbing a tree just to get a glimpse of hope. He didn't dismiss him—He called him by name.

Where others saw:

- Greed
- Reputation
- Contempt

Jesus saw:

- Hunger
- Curiosity
- A heart ready for repentance

Because Jesus saw beyond his wealth and sin, Zacchaeus experienced radical transformation—publicly and immediately.

Application

Do we look at the proud, the powerful, or the problematic and assume they're unreachable? Or do we have eyes to see the longing behind the mask?

> **3. He saw a sinner ready for salvation — The Thief on the Cross**
>
> **"Lord, remember me when thou comest into thy kingdom." —Luke 23:42 (KJV)**

As Jesus hung on the cross, two criminals flanked Him—both guilty. One mocked. The other cried out. And even in agony, Jesus saw a soul ready to be rescued.

He didn't say:

- "You're too late."
- "You're too far gone."
- "You've done too much."

He said:

> **"Today shalt thou be with me in paradise." —Luke 23:43 (KJV)**

That's vision: to see salvation where others see hopelessness.

Application

People may be moments from eternity, and we'll miss them unless we learn to see like Jesus.

The Church Must Pray for Eyes That See

> "Lift up your eyes, and look on the fields; for they are white already to harvest." —John 4:35 (KJV)

The harvest isn't coming—it's already here. But if we're not looking, we won't labor.

Signs our vision has died:

- We walk past broken people without praying.
- We assume some are "too far gone."
- We focus on outward success and miss spiritual emptiness.
- We fail to see everyday moments as divine appointments.

How to Regain Evangelistic Vision

1. Ask the Holy Spirit to anoint your eyes (see Ephesians 1:18).

2. Slow down to see people clearly.

3. Read the gospels regularly to see how Jesus saw.

4. Pray daily: *"Lord, open my eyes to the harvest."*

Don't Just Speak—See

Evangelism begins with seeing:

- The drunk neighbor as a potential preacher.
- The lonely teenager as a future leader.
- The hostile coworker as a heart waiting for healing.

When the church regains its vision, we won't need more programs; we'll need more laborers, because once we truly see the lost, we won't stay silent.

> **"Mine eye affecteth mine heart…" —Lamentations 3:51 (KJV)**

Let our eyes open again. Let our hearts break again. Let evangelism flow—because we see again.

> **"For the Son of man is come to seek and to save that which was lost." —Luke 19:10 (KJV)**

Zacchaeus didn't approach Jesus—Jesus approached Zacchaeus. That's the heart of evangelism: we go after them.

The Power of Personal Pursuit

Jesus didn't shout a sermon. He didn't call him out in judgment. He said:

> **"Zacchaeus, make haste, and come down; for to day I must abide at thy house." —Luke 19:5 (KJV)**

He made it personal. He gave dignity to a man who had only known rejection. The crowd grumbled, but Jesus prioritized presence over popularity.

Zacchaeus responded immediately. His heart was ready—he just needed someone to see him.

What We Learn from Jesus and Zacchaeus

1. Don't overlook the wealthy or powerful—they're often the loneliest.

2. Be willing to go to their space—Jesus went to his house.

3. Call people by name—evangelism is personal.

4. Expect transformation—Zacchaeus didn't just believe—he repented and restored.

"Behold, Lord, the half of my goods I give to the poor…" —Luke 19:8 (KJV)

A true encounter always brings fruit.

The Woman at the Well – Evangelism That Breaks Barriers

"Then cometh a woman of Samaria to draw water: Jesus saith unto her, give me to drink." —John 4:7 (KJV)

This woman was the wrong gender, the wrong race, and had the wrong past—according to culture. Most Jews avoided Samaria altogether. But not Jesus. He had to go through Samaria (John 4:4) because He had an appointment with a soul.

Jesus didn't just reach across a line—He shattered a wall.

Evangelism Confronts and Heals

He began with something simple: a request for water. Then He shifted the conversation toward eternity.

> **"Whosoever drinketh of this water shall thirst again: But whosoever drinketh of the water that I shall give…"** —John 4:14 (KJV)

He exposed her pain, but He didn't humiliate her. He revealed her sin, but He didn't reject her.

This is how Jesus evangelized:

- With truth that cut.
- With grace that healed.
- With wisdom that connected.

From Shame to Testimony

Her response was not shame—it was awakening. She left her waterpot—the very thing she came for—and ran back to town.

> **"Come, see a man, which told me all things that ever I did…"** —John 4:29 (KJV)

One woman became a voice. One conversation became a movement. Many in her city believed—because of her story.

What We Learn from Jesus and the Woman at the Well

1. Go where others won't—Jesus passed through rejected territory.

2. Start natural, go spiritual—He used water to talk about salvation.

3. Don't avoid the hard truth—He exposed her history with care.

4. Empower the transformed—Her testimony had power.

Evangelism is not just for the pulpit—it happens at wells, in moments, and through unlikely people.

The Thief on the Cross – Evangelism in the Final Hour

"And Jesus said unto him, Verily I say unto thee, To day shalt thou be with me in paradise." —Luke 23:43 (KJV)

As Jesus was dying, He was still reaching. Even in His final moments, He modeled what evangelism looks like: mercy, immediacy, and hope. Hanging next to Him was a man guilty by all accounts—a thief, a criminal, a reject of society. But Jesus saw beyond his record to his eternal value.

Salvation Is Always Within Reach

The thief simply said:

> **"Lord, remember me when thou comest into thy kingdom."**
> **—Luke 23:42 (KJV)**

It wasn't a perfect prayer. He didn't have time to clean up or make restitution. But it was sincere. And Jesus responded not with hesitation, but with certainty:

"To day shalt thou be with me…"

This was no probation—this was salvation.

No One Is Too Far Gone

This moment destroys every excuse we give for withholding the gospel:

- "It's too late for them."
- "They've made their choice."
- "They're too hardened."
- "They won't listen."

Jesus offers hope until the final breath. So must we.

What We Learn from Jesus and the Thief

1. Never assume it's too late—even the dying can be saved.

2. Be ready to witness in every moment—Jesus was in agony but still ministered.

3. Offer assurance—Evangelism must carry clarity, not confusion.

4. Look beyond behavior to brokenness—The thief wasn't asking for pity, but for grace.

Jesus didn't die alone. He took one more soul with Him to Paradise.

These three moments—Zacchaeus in the tree, the woman at the well, and the thief on the cross—show us that evangelism is not limited to time, place, or type of person. It is constant, personal, powerful, and urgent.

Philip the Evangelist – Spirit-Led, Word-Ready

Philip was led by the Spirit to the Ethiopian eunuch (Acts 8).

He:

- Listened to the Spirit.
- Obeyed without delay.
- Preached with clarity.
- Baptized with joy.

Philip shows that soul winners are Spirit-sensitive and Scripture-rooted.

Paul – Relentless in His Calling

From city to city, prison to platform, Paul never stopped preaching.

> **"…woe is unto me, if I preach not the gospel!" —1 Corinthians 9:16 (KJV)**

He shows us that true soul winners are driven not by comfort, but by conviction.

Modern-Day Soul Winners

Throughout history, God has used nameless men and women to turn cities upside down.

Evangelists, street preachers, missionaries, and ordinary believers have:

- Planted churches.
- Rescued addicts.
- Changed generations.

Profiles of Impact – Characters of Soul Winning Fire

These individuals—both biblical and modern—represent the kind of fire the church must rekindle. Their lives demonstrate the traits that should be present in every local body that seeks to reignite soul winning.

Jesus Christ – The Ultimate Soul Winner

He came to seek and save the lost (see Luke 19:10). He didn't just preach—He pursued. He didn't just gather crowds—He called individuals. Jesus modeled the balance of truth, grace, compassion, and urgency. Every evangelistic fire starts with Him.

The Samaritan Woman – From Outcast to Evangelist

In John 4, she encountered Jesus at the well and immediately became a soul winner. Though untrained and once rejected by society, her testimony sparked interest in an entire city. She shows that no title is required to impact lives—just transformation and testimony.

Philip the Evangelist – Spirit-Led and Ready

Philip didn't just go—he went when and where the Spirit led (see Acts 8). He didn't wait for a crowd; he reached one man in a chariot. Philip teaches us to obey the Spirit's timing and value each soul personally.

Paul the Apostle – Bold, Tireless, and Focused

Paul evangelized across cultures, endured beatings and imprisonment, and never lost sight of the mission. He didn't seek comfort—he pursued calling. His fire was fueled by a deep conviction that souls without Christ were eternally lost.

Peter – From Fearful to Fiery Preacher

After denying Christ, Peter was restored and became a fiery voice for the gospel at Pentecost. His transformation shows that failure doesn't disqualify you—it prepares you. The fire for souls is often born in the ashes of our own redemption.

Modern Evangelists (Collective Profile)

Throughout history and today, nameless missionaries, street preachers, campus ministers, and lay evangelists have burned with passion for the lost. They evangelize not for fame, but for fruit. They remind us that the fire is not confined to pulpits—it belongs in the streets.

They remind us that you don't need fame to be fruitful—just fire.

CHAPTER 14

THE REVIVAL THAT STARTS WITH REACHING ONE

"And he brought him to Jesus." —John 1:42 (KJV)

Evangelism can seem overwhelming when we think in terms of crowds. But revival doesn't start with a stadium—it starts with a single soul.

Andrew didn't preach at Pentecost—but he brought Peter to Jesus, and Peter's preaching saved thousands.

This chapter teaches that every soul matters and that revival begins one conversation, one act of obedience, one step at a time.

Every Soul Is a Seed

One soul won to Christ could lead to:

- A new family transformed.
- A future pastor or missionary saved.
- A ripple effect of impact.

Every Soul Is a Seed

"They that sow in tears shall reap in joy." —Psalm 126:5 (KJV)

Reigniting the Fire of Soul Winning in Our Churches

In the eyes of God, a single soul is never small. Every person you reach, every testimony you share, every gospel seed you plant carries eternal weight and multiplied potential. Because every soul saved is more than a statistic—it is a seed.

Just like a seed planted in good soil produces not just a tree, but fruit, shade, and more seeds, so too one soul saved can lead to generational transformation and worldwide impact.

The world measures numbers.

God measures fruit.

And when we win souls, we sow into a harvest we may never fully see—until eternity.

One Soul Can Transform an Entire Family

"Believe on the Lord Jesus Christ, and thou shalt be saved, and thy house." —Acts 16:31 (KJV)

When the Philippian jailer cried out, "What must I do to be saved?" Paul didn't just see one man—he saw a family tree. That night, his entire household was baptized (see Acts 16:33).

Every soul carries relational connections:

- Spouses
- Children
- Siblings
- Friends
- Co-workers

What if the person you lead to Christ today leads their entire family tomorrow? What if a single act of obedience opens the door to generational redemption?

You never just reach one person.

You reach everyone connected to that person.

One Soul Could Be a Future Leader—A Pastor, Missionary or Church Planter

"For ye see your calling, brethren… God hath chosen the foolish things of the world to confound the wise." —1 Corinthians 1:26–27 (KJV)

Evangelism is not just about bringing someone to heaven—it's about releasing someone into their kingdom calling. Many of today's pastors, missionaries, and evangelists were once:

- Addicts
- Atheists
- Prisoners
- Skeptics

Someone saw past their present and planted the seed of the gospel.

When Ananias prayed for Saul in Acts 9, he wasn't just helping a blind man—he was igniting the greatest missionary the world had ever seen.

Every soul is a Paul in process.

Every Seed Carries a Ripple Effect of Impact

> "Of the increase of his government and peace there shall be no end…" —Isaiah 9:7 (KJV)

The kingdom of God always expands. It is like leaven in the dough, a seed in the soil, or a fire in dry grass.

One soul leads to:

- One testimony.
- One changed household.
- One disciple-making movement.
- One ripple that affects nations.

Consider:

- Billy Graham was led to Christ by Mordecai Ham.
- D.L. Moody was saved through a faithful Sunday school teacher.
- Countless others were reached by unnamed laborers, but their seed produced global fruit.

You may not be famous, but your seed can shake nations.

Evangelism Must Be Vision-Driven, Not Just Event-Driven

> "The kingdom of heaven is like to a grain of mustard seed…" —Matthew 13:31 (KJV)

If you only see evangelism as an event, you'll measure success by how many people raised their hands. But if you see each soul as a seed, you'll labor with long-term vision and eternal hope.

Soul winning isn't about shallow conversions—it's about:

- Deep transformation.
- Long-term discipleship.
- Ongoing multiplication.

We don't just want professions of faith—we want fruit that remains.

> **"Ye have not chosen me, but I have chosen you… that ye should go and bring forth fruit, and that your fruit should remain…" —John 15:16 (KJV)**

The Church Must Be Seed-Conscious, Not Spotlight-Driven

The church must shift:

- From counting numbers to cultivating people.
- From pursuing fame to planting seeds.
- From temporary moments to eternal movements.

Every altar call is a planting moment.

Every outreach is a sowing season.

Every witness is a divine seed dropped into the soil of someone's soul.

We may water. We may not see the full harvest. But we must be faithful to plant.

Sow the Seed–And Expect a Harvest

"Let us not be weary in well doing: for in due season we shall reap, if we faint not."—Galatians 6:9 (KJV)

That person you're witnessing to may become a soul winner.

That child in your Sunday school may become a revivalist.

That one soul may become a thousand.

So keep planting. Keep preaching. Keep weeping. Keep reaching.

Because every soul is a seed.

And every seed contains a harvest.

"He that goeth forth and weepeth, bearing precious seed, shall doubtless come again with rejoicing, bringing his sheaves with him." —Psalm 126:6 (KJV)

"Despise not the day of small things…" —Zechariah 4:10 (paraphrased)

There is no such thing as an insignificant soul. Each one is a seed with eternal potential.

God Often Starts Small

- Jesus chose 12.
- The early church started in a room.
- Philip left a citywide revival to reach one eunuch.

The church must rediscover the power of personal evangelism. Revival doesn't wait for a crowd—it waits for a yes.

The Principle of Multiplication

"Go ye therefore, and teach all nations…" —Matthew 28:19 (KJV)

Jesus's model was reproducible. He poured into individuals who poured into others. The same fire that won you is meant to be passed on.

Teach your church this:

- Win one.
- Disciple one.
- Send one.

When multiplied, this simple process can turn the world upside down.

Never Underestimate the Power of One

Reignite your church's perspective. Don't overlook the single guest, the quiet neighbor, or the resistant co-worker. They may be the one.

"…likewise joy shall be in heaven over one sinner that repenteth…" —Luke 15:7 (KJV)

If heaven rejoices over one, so should we.

CHAPTER 15

RETURN TO THE MISSION

"As my Father hath sent me, even so send I you." —John 20:21 (KJV)

The church was never meant to drift from its assignment. Yet in many places today, the mission has been misplaced. We've traded the great commission for great productions, substituting the urgency of evangelism with the comfort of maintenance.

But God is calling His church back—not to busyness, but to purpose. Not to buildings, but to the broken. Not to programs, but to people. The church must return to its original mission: to seek and save the lost.

We've Drifted from the Call

"Nevertheless I have somewhat against thee, because thou hast left thy first love." —Revelation 2:4 (KJV)

The early church wasn't known for wealth, branding, or buildings. It was known for boldness, preaching, sacrifice, and salvation. The streets were their sanctuary. The poor were their congregation. The gospel was their only agenda.

Reigniting the Fire of Soul Winning in Our Churches

Today, many churches have become comfortable ships anchored in the harbor, when Jesus called us to be rescue boats launched into the storm.

The Mission Is Not Optional

> "Go ye therefore, and teach all nations…" —Matthew 28:19 (KJV)

This wasn't a suggestion or a side ministry—it was the central command of Christ. The church has no other legitimate reason for existing if it fails to carry out this directive.

To return to the mission means:

- Preaching the gospel again.
- Prioritizing lost souls over religious rituals.
- Discipling new believers intentionally.
- Training the whole church to reach the world.

It's Time to Mobilize, Not Entertain

> "And he called unto him the twelve, and began to send them forth two by two…" —Mark 6:7 (KJV)

Jesus didn't gather His followers just to sit in circles—He sent them out. He trained them to preach, pray, heal, and deliver. He called them into danger, not comfort. And He still sends us today.

We must return to a model where every believer is:

- Trained to share the gospel.

- Equipped to lead others to Christ.
- Commissioned to serve beyond the building.

The Church Must Be Sent Again

We don't just need church services—we need sent ones. The church must once again become a sending center:

- Sending believers into workplaces.
- Sending youth into their schools.
- Sending missionaries into neighborhoods.
- Sending witnesses into the streets.

> **"...how shall they hear without a preacher? And how shall they preach, except they be sent?" —Romans 10:14–15 (KJV)**

The time for spectatorship is over. The time for activation is now.

A Call to Return

We return to the mission when:

- We stop measuring church success by numbers and start measuring by impact.
- We stop keeping the saved comfortable and start reaching the lost with urgency.
- We stop building platforms and start building disciples.

> **"And daily in the temple, and in every house, they ceased not to teach and preach Jesus Christ." —Acts 5:42 (KJV)**

Church, it's time to return to the mission. The world is not waiting for another service—it's waiting for a Savior. And we've been entrusted with the message of His cross.

Return to the Altar

> **"And Elijah came unto all the people, and said, How long halt ye between two opinions?... And said Elijah unto all the people, Come near unto me... And he repaired the altar of the Lord that was broken down." —1 Kings 18:21, 30 (KJV)**

The altar is where the church began—and where it must return. Before there were microphones, lights, and stages, there were altars—places of prayer, sacrifice, and fire. But in too many modern churches, the altar has been replaced by atmosphere. Performance has replaced presence. The result? Emotion without encounter. Attendance without transformation. Movement without brokenness.

The call of God to the church today is simple and strong: Return to the altar.

The Altars Are Broken

In 1 Kings 18, the prophet Elijah stood on Mount Carmel confronting a nation that had turned to idolatry. But before the fire fell, he repaired the altar.

The altar of the Lord had been neglected and torn down. This is the prophetic picture of many churches today:

- Altar calls are rare or rushed.
- Prayer meetings are poorly attended.
- Conviction is minimized to avoid discomfort.

Yet it is at the altar that:

- Sins are confessed.
- Lives are surrendered.
- Fire is released.
- Callings are revived.

> **"If my people, which are called by my name, shall humble themselves, and pray…"** —2 Chronicles 7:14 (KJV)

There can be no revival without repentance. No fire without sacrifice. No evangelism without intercession. And no mission without an altar.

The Church Must Make Room Again

The altar must be restored as the centerpiece of the church—not just a piece of furniture at the front.

- Pastors must call people to repentance again.
- Leaders must model humility at the altar.
- Intercessors must return with travailing prayer.
- The people must once again approach God with awe, not just routine.

> **"...present your bodies a living sacrifice, holy, acceptable unto God, which is your reasonable service."**
> **—Romans 12:1 (KJV)**

The altar is not just a location—it's a lifestyle. It's where fire falls and where souls are drawn.

The Altar Prepares the Way for the Mission

A prayerless church will be a powerless church. The altar is not just for personal breakthrough—it's for corporate birthing.

Soul winning fire is born at the altar:

- Tears for the lost are wept here.
- Strategies for outreach are downloaded here.
- Burdens for cities are birthed here.
- Callings to go are heard here.

We must rebuild the altar in our services, in our homes, and in our hearts.

Return to the Altar

> **"Draw nigh to God, and he will draw nigh to you." — James 4:8 (KJV)**

When the altar is restored, God's presence returns. When the altar is restored, the people are awakened. When the altar is restored, the fire will fall again.

Church, return to the altar. It's time to rebuild.

CHAPTER 16

RETURN TO THE FIRE

> "…he shall baptize you with the Holy Ghost, and with fire." —Matthew 3:11 (KJV)

The church was born in fire. On the day of Pentecost, flames appeared on every head—not as a symbol, but as a sign of supernatural empowerment. The early church didn't need branding because they had boldness. They didn't need smoke machines because they carried spiritual fire.

But in many churches today, that fire has faded. The programs are polished, but the power is missing. The challenge is not that we need more resources—it's that we need more fire.

What the Fire Represents

1. **Purity – The fire of God cleanses.**

   > "…our God is a consuming fire." —Hebrews 12:29 (KJV)

It burns away compromise, lukewarmness, and sin.

2. **Passion – The fire fuels holy urgency.**

Reigniting the Fire of Soul Winning in Our Churches

> **"…his word was in mine heart as a burning fire shut up in my bones…" —Jeremiah 20:9 (KJV)**

It drives us to preach, pray, and pursue souls.

3. Power – The fire equips for mission.

> **"And there appeared unto them cloven tongues like as of fire… and they were all filled…" —Acts 2:3–4 (KJV)**

It releases boldness and miracles.

Without fire, churches become religious but fruitless. They may have form, but lack function.

The Fire Has Been Replaced in Many Churches

Instead of revival fire, we now have:

- Emotional hype.
- Entertaining sermons.
- Scheduled altar moments with no lingering.
- Outward activity with no inward power.

The Fire Has Been Replaced in Many Churches

> **"Having a form of godliness, but denying the power thereof: from such turn away." —2 Timothy 3:5 (KJV)**

The church is at a critical crossroads. In many places, we still have full schedules, packed services, and dynamic worship, but something vital is missing: the fire of God. We have maintained the appearance of revival, but lost the essence. We've settled for movement without power, and noise without transformation.

The fire of the Holy Spirit—the unmistakable presence that convicts, empowers, and sends—has too often been substituted with lesser things.

Emotional Hype Has Replaced Deep Conviction

It's possible to create an emotional atmosphere where people shout, cry, and dance—yet leave unchanged. Emotionalism is not the same as encounter.

— We clap, but don't consecrate.
— We cry, but don't crucify the flesh.
— We respond outwardly but don't repent inwardly.

"For godly sorrow worketh repentance to salvation…" —2 Corinthians 7:10 (KJV)

True fire produces godly sorrow, not just temporary feelings. But many churches now aim to stir emotion, not ignite transformation.

Entertaining Sermons Have Replaced Soul-Cutting Truth

Preaching today is often crafted more for applause than conviction. Pulpits have become platforms for inspiration, rather than altars of confrontation. **Sermons are more about:**

- Being relevant than being righteous.

- Making people feel better than making them right with God.
- Telling people what they want to hear rather than what they need to hear.

"Preach the word; be instant in season, out of season; reprove, rebuke, exhort…" —2 Timothy 4:2 (KJV)

The fire-filled sermons of the early church provoked people to cry out, "What must we do to be saved?" (see Acts 2:37). Today, many messages provoke laughter, inspiration, and applause—but rarely repentance.

Scheduled Altar Moments With No Lingering

In many churches today, altar calls have been reduced to quick gestures, tucked neatly into the service schedule to avoid discomfort or delay.

- People are asked to raise their hands, but not to lay down sin.
- We call for responses, but not for surrender.
- The altar is open, but the people are rushed.

"…tarry ye in the city of Jerusalem, until ye be endued with power from on high." —Luke 24:49 (KJV)

Power comes where there is lingering. Fire falls where there is waiting. But the modern church has grown impatient. We have services that move quickly, but don't move heaven.

Outward Activity Has Replaced Inward Power

Church calendars are full. Programs are polished. Events are excellent. But the presence of God cannot be scheduled, and revival cannot be programmed.

> **"Not by might, nor by power, but by my spirit, saith the Lord." —Zechariah 4:6 (KJV)**

You can have:

- Growth without godliness.
- Crowds without conversions.
- Influence without impact.
- Movement without miracles.

The church has busyness, but what we need is burning.

The Danger of a Fireless Church

A church without fire:

- Becomes institutional instead of inspirational.
- Focuses on comfort instead of consecration.
- Talks about the Spirit without walking in the Spirit.
- Avoids confrontation with culture to preserve reputation.

Jesus rebuked the Laodicean church for being lukewarm—not cold, not hot, but comfortable (see Revelation 3:15–17). Many churches today reflect the same temperature.

CHAPTER 17

A CALL BACK TO THE FIRE

The good news is this: the fire can fall again. But it will not come through performance—it will come through prayer. It won't come through more planning—but through repentance.

God is still looking for:

- Altars to consume.
- Churches that wait.
- Leaders who burn.
- Believers who live crucified.

> **"The fire shall ever be burning upon the altar; it shall never go out."** —Leviticus 6:13 (KJV)

The fire must return—not just to our services, but to our hearts.

How to Reignite the Fire

1. Preach repentance without apology.

2. Restore space in the altar for people to weep, linger, and be delivered.

3. Call the church back to prayer and fasting.

4. Eliminate performances and pursue presence.

5. Make room for the Holy Spirit to move without restriction.

Let us tear down the idols of hype, entertainment, and control. Let us rebuild the altars. Let us cry out for fire again. Because without it, we are nothing more than a religious machine with no eternal fruit.

"Quench not the Spirit." —1 Thessalonians 5:19 (KJV)

Church, the world does not need another program. It needs a church on fire.

But fire cannot be imitated. You can't fake the flame. Fire is heaven's endorsement. It's the mark of God's approval and power.

How to Return to the Fire

"Wherefore I put thee in remembrance that thou stir up the gift of God…" —2 Timothy 1:6 (KJV)

The fire doesn't rekindle itself—it must be stirred:

- Return to fasting and prayer.
- Preach with urgency again.
- Stop apologizing for the Holy Spirit.
- Cry out for fresh baptism and boldness.
- Allow the Spirit to move freely in every gathering.

Pastor Dr. Claudine Benjamin

The Fire Doesn't Rekindle Itself—It Must Be Stirred

"Wherefore I put thee in remembrance that thou stir up the gift of God, which is in thee…" —2 Timothy 1:6 (KJV)

Fire never keeps itself alive. If left untended, it dwindles. If ignored, it dies. This is true in the natural, and it's true spiritually. Many churches today wonder why the fire is gone, yet they've abandoned the disciplines that stoke the flame.

The Holy Spirit is ready to move. The fire is still available. But it must be stirred, fanned, and pursued with urgency.

Return to Fasting and Prayer

"This kind goeth not out but by prayer and fasting." — Matthew 17:21 (KJV)

Fasting and prayer are not spiritual extras—they are fire-starters. They align our hearts with heaven, crucify our flesh, and ignite our spirit.

Too many churches have reduced prayer to an opening ritual and abandoned fasting altogether. But the early church prayed with power and fasted with expectation.

— Prayer builds intimacy with God.
— Fasting breaks spiritual dullness.
— Together, they release spiritual power.

"Is not this the fast that I have chosen? … Then shall thy light break forth as the morning…" —Isaiah 58:6, 8 (KJV)

Reigniting the Fire of Soul Winning in Our Churches

To stir the fire, churches must return to corporate fasting, night watches, and prayer that groans for souls.

Preach With Urgency Again

"Cry aloud, spare not, lift up thy voice like a trumpet…" —Isaiah 58:1 (KJV)

Preaching in many pulpits today has lost its urgency. Messages are safe, polished, and practical—but where is the prophetic edge that awakens the dead and stirs the lukewarm?

We must return to preaching that:

- Confronts sin.
- Warns of judgment.
- Exalts Christ.
- Calls for repentance.
- Stirs a passion for souls.

Paul told Timothy to **"preach the word… in season, out of season."** (see 2 Timothy 4:2). That means with urgency, whether it's popular or not.

Preaching must regain its fire, not just to instruct minds, but to ignite hearts.

Stop Apologizing for the Holy Spirit

"And grieve not the holy Spirit of God…" —Ephesians 4:30 (KJV)

In many churches, the Holy Spirit has been reduced to a footnote. We mention Him, but we don't make room for Him. We fear offending people more than we fear grieving God.

- We stifle tongues.
- We ignore prophecy.
- We limit altar time.
- We avoid manifestations of power to remain "seeker-friendly."

But the Holy Spirit is not optional. He is the fire, the conviction, the boldness, and the power we desperately need.

"Quench not the Spirit." —1 Thessalonians 5:19 (KJV)

The church must stop apologizing and start honoring the Holy Spirit. He is not a disruption—He is the difference between religion and revival.

Cry Out for Fresh Baptism and Boldness

"And when they had prayed... they were all filled with the Holy Ghost, and they spake the word of God with boldness." —Acts 4:31 (KJV)

We don't just need more programs—we need a fresh outpouring. The baptism of the Holy Spirit is not a one-time event—it's a continual empowerment.

When the early church faced threats, they didn't retreat—they prayed for more boldness.

Today's church must cry out for:

Reigniting the Fire of Soul Winning in Our Churches

- Fresh fire.
- Fresh power.
- Fresh courage to confront darkness.
- Fresh baptism to go into all the world.

The harvest is too ripe, and the enemy too loud, for us to stay silent.

Allow the Spirit to Move Freely in Every Gathering

> "Now the Lord is that Spirit: and where the Spirit of the Lord is, there is liberty." —2 Corinthians 3:17 (KJV)

We've become experts in programming services down to the minute. But revival is not born in control—it's born in surrender.

- Allow time at the altar.
- Don't rush the response.
- Make room for prophetic flow.
- Prioritize presence over performance.

A church that limits the Spirit will eventually lose its flame. But a church that welcomes Him will walk in power, purity, and purpose.

> "...the glory of the Lord filled the house..." —2 Chronicles 5:14 (KJV)

Let His glory come again—not as a concept, but as a consuming reality.

Stir the Fire Again

- Let pastors stir it in the pulpit.
- Let intercessors stir it in the prayer room.
- Let worshippers stir it with hunger.

- Let every believer take personal responsibility to guard and grow the fire.

Because fire doesn't rekindle itself—it must be stirred.

> **"Neglect not the gift that is in thee... meditate upon these things; give thyself wholly to them..." —1 Timothy 4:14–15 (KJV)**

If we stir the flame, God will send the fire.

Churches that burn with fire:
- Drive out apathy.
- Birth revival.
- Fill the altars.

Return to Fasting and Prayer – Rekindling Intimacy with God

> **"Is not this the fast that I have chosen?" —Isaiah 58:6 (KJV)**

When the early church prayed, heaven responded. When they fasted, power was released. In today's fast-paced, comfort-driven Christianity, fasting and prayer are often neglected or viewed as optional. But if we want to rekindle the fire of evangelism, we must first return to the altar of consecration.

Fasting and prayer clear spiritual clutter and sharpen spiritual hearing. **These disciplines:**

- Break strongholds (see Isaiah 58:6).

- Restore sensitivity to the Holy Spirit.
- Birth boldness to proclaim truth.

Fasting and Prayer—Clearing the Clutter for the Harvest

> **"Is not this the fast that I have chosen? to loose the bands of wickedness, to undo the heavy burdens… and that ye break every yoke?" —Isaiah 58:6 (KJV)**

In a world flooded with distractions and spiritual noise, one thing is absolutely clear: if the church is going to hear from God, she must remove the clutter and return to the discipline of fasting and prayer.

These are not outdated practices. They are battle-tested weapons—God-ordained strategies to:

- Break spiritual bondage.
- Recover clarity.
- Ignite boldness.
- Unlock divine harvest strategies.

Fasting and prayer silences the chaos and tune the believer's ear to heaven's frequency.

Fasting and Prayer Break Strongholds

> **"This kind can come forth by nothing, but by prayer and fasting." —Mark 9:29 (KJV)**

Some spiritual resistance doesn't move through teaching or singing. Some strongholds—especially those resisting revival and evangelism—must be broken through fasting and prayer.

Whether personal or regional, fasting:

- Exposes hidden oppression.
- Weakens demonic footholds.
- Breaks generational cycles.
- Reclaims territory in the spirit realm.

Isaiah 58:6 declares fasting is God's tool to "loose the bands of wickedness." It's not just about discipline—it's about deliverance. The enemy may withstand your efforts, but he cannot withstand your consecration.

If a city is bound in darkness, call a fast. If your evangelism feels resisted, go into prayer. If hearts are hardened, press in until the yoke breaks.

Fasting and Prayer Restore Sensitivity to the Holy Spirit

> **"As they ministered to the Lord, and fasted, the Holy Ghost said…" —Acts 13:2 (KJV)**

When the church stops hearing, it's because she's filled with too much noise. Fasting stills the soul. Prayer clears the static. Together, they tune your spiritual ears to the whisper of the Spirit.

When you're spiritually sensitive:

Reigniting the Fire of Soul Winning in Our Churches

- You know where to go.
- You know when to speak.
- You know whom to reach.
- You know how to respond.

Paul and Barnabas were launched into ministry through a word received during a fast (see Acts 13). Evangelistic clarity flows from a quieted heart.

Application

If your hearing feels dull, go into fasting. Make space for silence. Let God speak again.

Fasting and Prayer Birth Boldness to Proclaim Truth

"And when they had fasted and prayed… they sent them away." —Acts 13:3 (KJV)

The early church didn't send out messengers with cute messages—they sent out burning ones filled with power, courage, and conviction. That boldness wasn't natural. It came from spiritual discipline.

Prayer and fasting strip the fear of man. They fill you with:

- Heaven's burden.
- Heaven's message.
- Heaven's fire.

Fasting makes you confront your own weaknesses and excuses. Prayer fills you with holy courage to speak truth, even when it's unpopular.

> "And when they had prayed, the place was shaken... and they were all filled with the Holy Ghost, and spake the word of God with boldness." —Acts 4:31 (KJV)

Application

When evangelism becomes timid and hesitant, it's time to birth boldness on your knees.

Fasting and Prayer Release Divine Strategies for the Harvest

> "Call unto me, and I will answer thee, and show thee great and mighty things, which thou knowest not." — Jeremiah 33:3 (KJV)

The harvest requires more than good ideas—it requires God's insight. Where should we go? How should we reach them? Who is God targeting next?

These answers come not from meetings, but from intercession.

In prayer and fasting, God releases:

- Supernatural evangelism plans.
- Specific people and places to target.
- Timing for revivals and outreaches.
- Prophetic words that unlock hearts.

Reigniting the Fire of Soul Winning in Our Churches

Fasting aligns the church with heaven's agenda.

Application

Before you plan your next outreach, call a fast. Get the blueprint from the Holy Spirit.

Consecrate to Conquer

> **"Sanctify a fast, call a solemn assembly… and cry unto the Lord." —Joel 1:14 (KJV)**

The church will not win this war in the flesh. We will not reclaim cities with surface-level prayers and casual gatherings.

We need:

- Fasting that breaks chains.
- Prayer that shakes altars.
- Sensitivity that hears God's whisper.
- Boldness that challenges darkness.
- Strategies that come straight from heaven.

Fasting and prayer aren't side tools—they are essential weapons for soul winners. If you want to see revival in the streets, you must first birth it in the secret place.

> "…when ye fast…" —Matthew 6:16

Not if—when.

> **"But thou, when thou fastest, anoint thine head, and wash thy face… and thy Father, which seeth in secret, shall reward thee openly." —Matthew 6:17–18 (KJV)**

Jesus didn't say if you fast—He said when.

A fireless church is often a prayerless church. A church without fasting becomes a church with no fire on the altar.

Preach with Urgency Again – Restoring the Weight of the Word

> **"Preach the word; be instant in season, out of season…" —2 Timothy 4:2 (KJV)**

The pulpit is not a platform for performance—it is a launchpad for mission. Preaching is not for applause but for awakening. When preachers stop preaching with urgency, the church stops responding with urgency.

The early apostles didn't preach to impress—they preached to rescue souls from eternal destruction.

Today, we must return to:

- Preaching sin as sin.
- Declaring that hell is real.
- Pointing boldly to the cross.
- Calling clearly for repentance.
- Speaking prophetically, not politically.

> **"Knowing therefore the terror of the Lord, we persuade men…"** —2 Corinthians 5:11 (KJV)

Urgent preaching comes from a heart on fire. If the pulpit is casual, the pew will be complacent.

We must raise our voices—not to entertain, but to warn and win.

Stop Apologizing for the Holy Spirit – Let God Move Freely Again

> **"Quench not the Spirit."** —1 Thessalonians 5:19 (KJV)

In too many places, the Holy Spirit has been treated like an uninvited guest—acknowledged but not welcomed. His gifts are restricted. His power is avoided. His movement is confined to carefully scheduled services.

But the church was born in fire because it welcomed the Spirit without restriction.

We must stop:

- Explaining Him away to please visitors.
- Silencing tongues to avoid offense.
- Controlling services to maintain appearances.
- Downplaying manifestations of the Spirit.

> **"…where the Spirit of the Lord is, there is liberty."**—2 Corinthians 3:17 (KJV)

If we want revival, we must allow the Holy Spirit to take the lead.

We do not need more polished programs. We need:

- Prophetic interruptions.
- Divine manifestations.
- Supernatural boldness.
- Glory that transforms.

God will not send His fire where He is not free to reign.

Return to Fasting and Prayer – The Forgotten Fuel of Revival

"…this kind goeth not out but by prayer and fasting." — Matthew 17:21 (KJV)

Fasting and prayer are not old-fashioned—they are foundational. The early church was birthed in an atmosphere of both (see Acts 1:14 and 13:2-3). Where prayer is fervent and fasting is practiced, the fire of God falls.

In today's culture, churches are often marked by events, social media, and strategy sessions—but rarely by extended prayer meetings or corporate fasts. Yet every great revival in history was preceded by deep travailing in prayer and sacrificial fasting.

Why Fasting and Prayer Matters

- They break the power of the flesh.
- They align our will with God's.
- They sharpen our spiritual discernment.

- They release supernatural intervention (see Isaiah 58:6–11).

> **"…call a solemn assembly… let the priests, the ministers of the Lord, weep between the porch and the altar…" — Joel 2:15–17 (KJV)**

God is not looking for more charisma—He's looking for consecration.

How to Restore Fasting and Prayer in the Church

- Set regular church-wide prayer and fasting days.
- Teach on biblical fasting—show that it's a lifestyle, not a punishment.
- Create prayer altars and teams that go beyond Sunday.
- Fast not just for personal breakthrough—but for citywide revival.

When churches return to fasting and prayer, they return to power.

Preach with Urgency Again - Sound the Alarm

> **"Blow ye the trumpet in Zion… let all the inhabitants of the land tremble: for the day of the Lord cometh…" — Joel 2:1 (KJV)**

Preaching has lost its urgency in many pulpits. We've traded the trumpet for a microphone—and silenced the alarm.

But we are not motivational speakers—we are messengers of the King. The Word must once again be preached:

- With fire.
- With tears.
- With boldness.
- With the urgency of eternity.

Why Urgent Preaching Is Needed

- Hell is real

  "Where their worm dieth not, and the fire is not quenched." —Mark 9:44 (KJV).

- Jesus is coming soon

  "The night is far spent, the day is at hand..." — Romans 13:12 (KJV).

- The harvest is perishing

  "The harvest is past, the summer is ended, and we are not saved." —Jeremiah 8:20 (KJV)

The preacher must stop entertaining and start evangelizing.

Let Preaching Cut Again

"Now when they heard this, they were pricked in their heart..." —Acts 2:37 (KJV)

Anointed preaching pierces, convicts, and draws people to repentance. We need preaching that awakens the lukewarm and saves the lost.

Churches that preach with urgency become churches that harvest with consistency.

Stop Apologizing for the Holy Spirit – Make Room for the Fire

> **"Grieve not the Holy Spirit of God…" —Ephesians 4:30 (KJV)**

The modern church often treats the Holy Spirit like an embarrassing relative—acknowledging Him, but carefully avoiding any visible demonstration of His power. But the Holy Spirit is not optional—He is essential.

When we apologize for Him, we offend the very One who empowers us.

What Happens When We Quench the Spirit

- The fire dies out.
- Miracles become rare.
- Evangelism becomes mechanical.
- Services lack conviction.

What Happens When We Quench the Spirit

> **"Quench not the Spirit." —1 Thessalonians 5:19 (KJV)**

The Holy Spirit is not a force to be manipulated. He is the third person of the Trinity, the divine presence of God among His people. He is holy. He is sensitive. And when He is welcomed, fire falls, chains break, and revival flows. But when He is quenched, everything changes.

To quench the Spirit means to suppress, extinguish, or resist His movements. And while we may still gather, sing, and preach, a quenched Spirit leads to a powerless church.

The Fire Dies Out

"The fire shall ever be burning upon the altar; it shall never go out." —Leviticus 6:13 (KJV)

The fire of the Spirit is not sustained by skill or schedule—it is sustained by surrender. When we quench the Spirit, we cut off the oxygen to the flame. The passion fades. The hunger wanes. The altar grows cold.

When the fire of soul winning dies, the church becomes a shell of its calling:

- Preaching becomes passionless.
- Worship becomes predictable.
- Prayer becomes mechanical.
- Services become routine.
- We stop reaching.
- We start entertaining.

In the absence of fire, souls remain lost. But all is not lost. God is calling the church back to the fire, and He is raising up a generation of soul winning reformers—those who will not just attend church, but ignite it.

Here are five symbolic characters who show us both the decline and the path to reigniting the fire of soul winning.

Reigniting the Fire of Soul Winning in Our Churches

1. Pastor Eli – The Passionless Preacher

Eli once preached with fire. His altar was full, and his tears flowed as he called sinners home. But over time, he started performing. He still studied. He still preached. But his passion waned.

He no longer wept over the lost—he wept over empty seats and low offering reports.

He represents the pastor who kept the routine but lost the burden.

But God visited him in a dream—showing him the people he passed every day who had never heard the gospel.

He woke up burning again. He repented publicly. And when he preached again, he wasn't performing—he was pleading.

Fire returned. And so did souls.

2. Sister Lora – The Predictable Worship Leader

Lora could sing heaven down. Her voice was powerful, and her songs were polished. But over time, worship became about setlists and transitions, not tears and surrender.

She stopped praying before services. She stopped listening for what God wanted sung. Worship became predictable. Safe. Stylish. But shallow.

Then one Sunday, she saw a visitor—eyes filled with pain—leave before the altar call. That image broke her. That night, she stayed at the altar for hours, crying, *"God, give me my sensitivity back!"*

He did. And her worship changed. She started singing prophetically. The atmosphere shifted. People began getting saved during songs.

Worship without soul winning is noise. Worship with a burden brings glory.

3. Deacon Miles – The Mechanical Prayer Warrior

Miles used to pray with fire. He travailed. He fasted. But now his prayers were time slots, not encounters. He opened prayer meetings with cold formality. No tears. No warfare. Just tradition.

Then his teenage son confessed he didn't believe in God. The news shattered Miles. That night, he returned to the closet. Not for a scheduled prayer—but for a desperate cry.

He wept. He shouted. He groaned. He rebuked darkness over his family. That night, prayer returned—and power followed.

The next week, people at the prayer meeting were being delivered. Conviction returned. Souls were drawn back to Christ.

Dead prayer meetings don't shake hell. Fiery ones do.

4. Sister Grace – The Silent Intercessor Who Reignited the Church

Grace had no title. No mic. But she had fire. While others grew cold, she stayed burning. Every Sunday, she walked the sanctuary—anointing seats, praying for sinners, calling out names in the spirit.

She'd fast for days. She'd weep during worship. She'd intercede when no one else showed up.

One day, revival broke out in the church. The pastor asked, *"Who's been crying out for this?"* Grace sat in the back, hands lifted, silent. She didn't need credit—she carried the fire.

Sometimes the loudest revival doesn't start on the platform—it starts in the prayer closet.

5. Jordan – The Young Evangelist Who Refused to Play Church

Jordan was 19. Newly saved. Unpolished. Untrained. But ablaze.

He wasn't interested in youth trips or merch tables—he wanted the gospel. Every Friday, he preached downtown. Every Sunday, he brought five or six new people. Some came high. Some came homeless. All came hungry.

The church leaders weren't sure what to do with him. He didn't "fit the culture." But they couldn't deny the fruit.

His fire began to convict the rest of the church. Soon, the youth group turned into a prayer furnace. Bible studies birthed street outreaches. His flame spread like wildfire.

Soul winners don't wait for permission. They obey the great commission.

We Can't Afford Cold Churches in a Dying World

If we don't reignite the fire of soul winning, preaching becomes a performance.

> **"Preach the word; be instant in season, out of season..."**
> **—2 Timothy 4:2 (KJV)**

Preaching without the fire of soul winning becomes a show. Messages are crafted to impress, not convict. Sermons aim to entertain, not evangelize. The pulpit becomes a stage, and the gospel is replaced by self-help, clichés, and cultural appeasement.

A fireless preacher:

- Fears offending more than he fears God.
- Avoids truth to attract crowds.
- Prioritizes applause over altar calls.

When the Fire Returns, Conviction Comes Back

> **"And when he is come, he will reprove the world of sin, and of righteousness, and of judgment." —John 16:8 (KJV)**

Conviction is not condemnation—it's the voice of a holy God calling people back to Himself. When the fire of the Holy Spirit returns, conviction floods the atmosphere.

People don't just hear truth—they are pierced by it.

They don't just sing about grace—they run to receive it.

Reigniting the Fire of Soul Winning in Our Churches

They don't just attend church—they meet God there.

Without fire, the Word can be heard and ignored. But with fire:

- Sin is exposed.
- Hearts are broken.
- Repentance becomes immediate.
- People fall to their knees without an altar call.

Cold churches dismiss sin. Fiery churches drive people to the cross.

Conviction isn't offensive—it's essential for soul winning.

When the Fire Returns, Urgency Is Restored

"Knowing therefore the terror of the Lord, we persuade men…" —2 Corinthians 5:11 (KJV)

One of the first things to die when the fire leaves is urgency. Churches settle into maintenance mode. Sermons become safe. Evangelism is postponed.

But when the fire returns, the church is awakened to the urgency of eternity. Time is short. Hell is real. Heaven is near. And souls must be reached now.

Fiery urgency sounds like:

- "We must go out today."
- "We can't delay obedience."
- "Someone's eternity depends on this."

- "If not now—when?"

The early church didn't have buildings, budgets, or branding. But they had urgency, and they turned the world upside down.

> **"I must work the works of him that sent me, while it is day…" —John 9:4 (KJV)**

Fire restores urgency—and urgency fuels soul winning.

When the Fire Returns, Tears Begin to Flow Again

> **"They that sow in tears shall reap in joy." —Psalm 126:5 (KJV)**

A sign of a cold church is dry altars. No weeping. No brokenness. Just polite attendance and quick exits. But when the fire returns, tears come back.

Not tears of emotion—but tears of:

- Repentance
- Intercession
- Compassion for the lost
- Hunger for God

Tears are a language heaven understands. They water revival. They soften hearts. They break pride.

When the fire returns:

Reigniting the Fire of Soul Winning in Our Churches

- Men cry again.
- Children weep at the altar.
- Intercessors groan in the Spirit.
- Pastors break over their pulpits.

Tears are not weakness—they're evidence of a holy burden.

A tearless church will never reach a bleeding world.

When the Fire Returns, Deliverance Is Activated

"And these signs shall follow them that believe; In my name shall they cast out devils…" —Mark 16:17 (KJV)

Without fire, people learn how to cope with bondage.

With fire, they are set free from it.

Deliverance isn't just a ministry—it's the overflow of fiery presence. When the Holy Spirit is welcomed and the gospel is preached with power:

- Chains break.
- Addictions are severed.
- Depression lifts.
- Demons flee.

A cold church explains symptoms. A fiery church confronts the spirit behind it.

Jesus never left people as He found them. The early church didn't just inform—they delivered. And today, God is still raising up deliverers—not just with microphones, but with mantles.

No fire—no freedom. Fireless churches create religious captives.

When the Fire Returns, Transformation Happens

> "...be ye transformed by the renewing of your mind..."
> **—Romans 12:2 (KJV)**

Real transformation doesn't happen through good advice. It happens through God encounters. When fire fills the church again, people don't just cry—they change.

They leave different:

- Addicts become intercessors.
- Abusers become apostles.
- Atheists become evangelists.
- The bitter become burdened for souls.

Programs can't do this. Polished presentations can't do this. Only fire can burn away the old and birth the new.

When the fire returns:

- Marriages are restored.
- Families are saved.
- Generations are healed.

Reigniting the Fire of Soul Winning in Our Churches

- The unsaved are converted—not persuaded, but transformed.

Fire doesn't just warm—it reshapes. It refines. It revives.

The Church Must Burn Again

We've had enough:

- Performance without power.
- Music without anointing.
- Preaching without passion.
- Services without souls.

The church doesn't need more polish. It needs more presence. It needs fire.

> **"…he shall baptize you with the Holy Ghost, and with fire." —Matthew 3:11 (KJV)**

Let the fire fall. Let conviction return. Let urgency rise. Let tears flow. Let deliverance break out. Let transformation shake the city. When the fire returns, so does everything the enemy tried to steal.

> **"Is not my word like as a fire? saith the Lord…" — Jeremiah 23:29 (KJV)**

When preaching burns again, souls will return to the altar.

When Worship Becomes Empty

"This people draweth nigh unto me with their mouth, and honoureth me with their lips; but their heart is far from me." —Matthew 15:8 (KJV)

Worship disconnected from soul winning becomes shallow and self-centered. We sing with hands raised but hearts closed. The songs are loud, but the altars are silent. People feel goosebumps—but not God.

Signs of empty worship:

- No altar response.
- No tears.
- No repentance.
- No hunger for holiness.

But when the fire of evangelistic passion returns:

- Worship moves from emotionalism to encounter.
- Hearts are softened.
- The presence of God draws the lost.
- Songs carry prophetic urgency.

When worship is alive, lost souls are awakened.

When Prayer Becomes Passive

"The effectual fervent prayer of a righteous man availeth much." —James 5:16b (KJV)

Reigniting the Fire of Soul Winning in Our Churches

Prayer without evangelistic fire becomes routine, shallow, and powerless. Churches pray for blessings, comfort, and favor—but not for souls, repentance, or revival.

Cold prayer meetings produce:

- Cold services.
- Cold hearts.
- Cold altars.

When the church stops weeping for the lost, it starts dying.

But when prayer is reignited:

- Intercessors rise.
- Altars are filled.
- Spiritual warfare is waged.
- Souls are snatched from hell.

Evangelism begins on your knees before it begins in the streets.

When Church Becomes Forgettable

"Ichabod... the glory is departed." —1 Samuel 4:21 (KJV)

Church without fire becomes irrelevant. People attend, but don't transform. They leave talking about the lights and transitions, not about the presence of God or the power of the gospel.

Forgettable churches:

- Focus on branding more than burden.
- Entertain believers instead of equipping soul winners.
- Avoid altar calls to keep services short and "friendly."

But when the fire returns:

- Atmospheres shift.
- Conviction falls.
- The presence of God becomes tangible.
- Unbelievers cry out for salvation.

"And when he is come, he will reprove the world of sin, and of righteousness, and of judgment." —John 16:8 (KJV)

The church must be unforgettable, because eternity is at stake.

When the Lost Stay Lost

"Say not ye, There are yet four months… lift up your eyes, and look on the fields…" —John 4:35 (KJV)

The most tragic result of a cold church is this: the lost remain lost. While we debate doctrine, polish programs, and upgrade production, souls are slipping into eternity without Christ.

A cold church is not harmless—it's dangerous.

Reigniting the Fire of Soul Winning in Our Churches

When the church loses her burden:

- Hell enlarges.
- Heaven weeps.
- The great commission is abandoned.

But when soul winning is reignited:

- The church is mobilized.
- The gospel is preached.
- The lost are found.
- Heaven rejoices.

"...he that winneth souls is wise." —Proverbs 11:30 (KJV)

The church cannot be casual about what God takes seriously.

Let the Fire Fall Again

We can no longer afford cold pulpits, worship, prayers, and churches while the world is burning and souls are dying. Reignite the fire. Rekindle the passion. Restore the urgency.

When the church is ablaze with the burden for souls, revival becomes inevitable.

But if we return to the fire:

- Altar calls overflow.
- Salvations multiply.
- Deliverance erupts.

- Worship breaks yokes.

> **"He that goeth forth and weepeth, bearing precious seed, shall doubtless come again with rejoicing..."** —Psalm 126:6 (KJV)

Let the passion return.
Let the burden burn.
Let the church rise again—with fire for the lost.
Reignite the soul winners. Reignite the flame. Let the fire fall—and let it spread.

Many churches still meet, but the fire is gone. Why? Because the Spirit has been boxed out by control, fear, pride, or performance.

Application

The fire cannot fall where control reigns. If we want the fire back, we must welcome the Spirit back.

When Miracles Become Rare

> **"And he did not many mighty works there because of their unbelief."** —Matthew 13:58 (KJV)

When the Spirit is quenched, the supernatural becomes scarce. Healing stops. Deliverance disappears. Prophetic insight fades. Services become explainable, manageable, and void of divine interruption.

Reigniting the Fire of Soul Winning in Our Churches

The early church saw miracles not because they were perfect, but because they were yielded. They prayed, fasted, obeyed, and allowed the Spirit to interrupt their plans.

But today:

- Many churches resist spiritual gifts.
- Miracles are explained away.
- We rely on medicine, not intercession.
- We preach healing without faith to see it.

Quenching the Spirit removes the atmosphere where heaven touches earth.

Application

If miracles are missing, ask: *"Have we made room for the Spirit to move?"*

Evangelism Becomes Mechanical

> **"And when they had prayed, the place was shaken where they were assembled together; and they were all filled with the Holy Ghost, and they spake the word of God with boldness." —Acts 4:31 (KJV)**

Without the Spirit, evangelism becomes a chore, not a calling. It becomes a checkbox on a church program instead of a burden on a believer's heart.

When the Spirit is quenched:

- Boldness evaporates.
- The burden for the lost disappears.
- Conviction is absent.
- Compassion is shallow.

We can still hand out tracts or run outreaches, but without the Spirit, we lack fire, insight, and supernatural guidance. Evangelism becomes a formula, not a flame.

Application

The Spirit breathes fire into your witness. If soul winning feels dead, ask for a fresh infilling.

When Services Lack Conviction

"And when he is come, he will reprove the world of sin, and of righteousness, and of judgment." —John 16:8 (KJV)

The Holy Spirit is the source of conviction. He doesn't shame—He awakens. When the Spirit is active, people don't leave the same. **They leave:**

- Changed
- Challenged
- Chosen
- Clean

The Holy Spirit Is the Source of Conviction—Not Shame

> **"And when he is come, he will reprove the world of sin, and of righteousness, and of judgment." —John 16:8 (KJV)**

There is a holy weight that enters a room when the Holy Spirit begins to move. It is not emotional hype. It is not manipulation. It is not guilt.

It is conviction—a divine awakening that reveals the truth of our condition, the nearness of God's mercy, and the urgency of surrender.

The Holy Spirit never condemns the believer. He does not humiliate the sinner. He does not push people away from God—He draws them to the cross. Conviction is a gift, not a punishment.

Where the Holy Spirit is free to work, people leave the presence of God:

- Changed in heart.
- Challenged in behavior.
- Chosen in purpose.
- Clean in spirit.

Conviction Brings Change—Not Just Emotion

> **"Now when they heard this, they were pricked in their heart..." —Acts 2:37 (KJV)**

On the day of Pentecost, Peter didn't preach a motivational message. He preached truth in fire—and the crowd didn't leave entertained. They left transformed.

The Spirit cut through their hearts and brought them to repentance. That is what true conviction does: it doesn't make you cry just to cry—it changes you.

Conviction leads to:

- Immediate repentance.
- Public confession.
- Genuine transformation.
- Fruit that remains.

If people keep leaving services the same way they came in, it's not because the Spirit isn't available—it's often because He's been quenched or ignored.

Conviction Challenges What We've Tolerated

> "For the word of God is quick, and powerful... a discerner of the thoughts and intents of the heart." — **Hebrews 4:12 (KJV)**

True conviction confronts compromise. The Holy Spirit challenges what you've made peace with—whether it's hidden sin, spiritual laziness, unforgiveness, or pride.

He doesn't whisper affirmations over rebellion. He lovingly shines light on the areas we've tucked away.

He challenges you to:

- Forgive when you want to be bitter.
- Confess what you've tried to hide.
- Obey when it's inconvenient.
- Walk holy when the crowd walks casually.

And He does it not with cruelty, but with clarity and love.

> "As many as I love, I rebuke and chasten: be zealous therefore, and repent." —Revelation 3:19 (KJV)

Conviction Reveals That We Are Chosen, Not Rejected

> "No man can come to me, except the Father… draw him." —John 6:44 (KJV)

Conviction is not a sign that God is rejecting you—it's proof that He's pursuing you. The Holy Spirit doesn't awaken your conscience to condemn you, but to call you.

He is saying:

- "You were made for more."
- "There's grace for your failure."
- "I'm not finished with you yet."
- "I chose you—now choose Me."

Conviction Is a Call, Not a Condemnation

"For whom the Lord loveth he correcteth; even as a father the son in whom he delighteth." —Proverbs 3:12 (KJV)

If you feel the weight of conviction today, you are not being rejected—you are being reached. The enemy wants you to think conviction is a sign you've failed too badly to be used. But in reality, it's the evidence that God is not finished with you.
Conviction is not a weapon of shame—it is the whisper of the Spirit, inviting you back to the place where grace restores, healing flows, and purpose is reignited.

Conviction Says: "You Were Made for More"

"Before I formed thee in the belly I knew thee; and before thou camest forth out of the womb I sanctified thee…" —Jeremiah 1:5 (KJV)

Sin shrinks our sense of identity. It blinds us to who we really are and distorts what we were born to do. But the Holy Spirit doesn't let you settle. He convicts not just to show you what's wrong, but to remind you of who you are.

He's not yelling in disappointment. He's calling you higher:

- Out of the pit of addiction.
- Out of the fog of confusion.
- Out of the prison of shame.
- Into the truth of your God-given design.

Every time the Spirit convicts, He's saying, *"You were made for more than this compromise, this habit, this hiding. Come up higher."*

Conviction Says: "There's Grace for Your Failure"

> **"But where sin abounded, grace did much more abound." —Romans 5:20 (KJV)**

Conviction never comes without a path to mercy. That's the difference between the enemy's voice and the Holy Spirit's. Satan condemns to destroy. The Spirit convicts to deliver.

When Peter denied Jesus three times, he wept bitterly. But Jesus didn't remove him—He restored him. In John 21, He called Peter back with grace and gave him his assignment again: "Feed My sheep."

When the Spirit convicts you, He's not writing you off. He's reminding you: "My grace is sufficient" (see 2 Corinthians 12:9).

He's not focused on your fall—He's focused on your comeback.

Conviction Says: "I'm Not Finished With You Yet"

> **"Being confident of this very thing, that he which hath begun a good work in you will perform it..." — Philippians 1:6 (KJV)**

God never starts a story He doesn't intend to finish. And conviction is proof that your story is still being written.

It doesn't matter:

- How far you've drifted.
- How long you've wandered.
- How deep you've fallen.

If you can still hear His voice, then you're not disqualified—you're being drawn back. The Spirit doesn't show up to say, "You're done." He shows up to say, "I'm still working."

If God had given up on you, you wouldn't feel convicted—you'd feel nothing. But because you still feel His tug, you're still His.

Conviction Says: "I Chose You—Now Choose Me"

> **"Ye have not chosen me, but I have chosen you, and ordained you…" —John 15:16 (KJV)**

Conviction is God knocking at the door of your heart again, reminding you of a divine relationship that He initiated, but that you must now respond to.

He chose you before the foundation of the world. He designed your calling. He reserved a seat at His table with your name on it. And now He's saying:

- "Come home."
- "Choose truth."
- "Choose healing."
- "Choose Me."

This is not guilt. It's grace calling your name.

Reigniting the Fire of Soul Winning in Our Churches

And once you choose Him back, everything changes:

- Guilt gives way to peace.
- Shame gives way to boldness.
- Aimlessness gives way to destiny.

The Enemy Condemns, but the Spirit Calls

"There is therefore now no condemnation to them which are in Christ Jesus…" —Romans 8:1 (KJV)

— Condemnation says, "You're unworthy, unwanted, unusable."
— Conviction says, "You're called, cleansed, and chosen."

The enemy wants you to believe the Holy Spirit comes to crush you. But in truth, the Spirit comes to carry you out of darkness into freedom.

When conviction hits your heart, it's not to push you away from God—it's to pull you closer.

When Conviction Comes—Respond

You don't need to hide.
You don't need to pretend.
You don't need to perform.
You just need to say: "Yes, Lord. I hear You. I choose You back."

Because:

- You were made for more.

- There's grace for your failure.
- He's not finished with you.
- He chose you—now choose Him.

"Behold, I stand at the door, and knock…" —Revelation 3:20 (KJV)

Conviction is the knock.
Grace is the invitation.
Freedom is waiting on the other side.

The enemy uses guilt to drive people away from God. The Spirit uses conviction to bring them back to God.

Even when conviction is heavy, the undertone is always hope.

"For godly sorrow worketh repentance to salvation not to be repented of…" —2 Corinthians 7:10 (KJV)

Conviction Cleanses and Restores

"Create in me a clean heart, O God; and renew a right spirit within me." —Psalm 51:10 (KJV)

When the Holy Spirit convicts, He doesn't just expose your sin—He cleanses you from it. He doesn't just show you the stain—He offers the soap of grace.

The result of conviction is:

- A clear conscience.

- A renewed spirit.
- Joy restored.
- Peace returning.

Conviction That Cleanses—Not Condemns

"Come now, and let us reason together, saith the Lord: though your sins be as scarlet, they shall be as white as snow…" —Isaiah 1:18 (KJV)

The Holy Spirit is not in the business of condemnation—He's in the business of cleansing. He doesn't just expose what's wrong—He makes it right. He doesn't humiliate—He heals.

Conviction is not God pointing a finger in anger. It is God extending His hand in mercy.

When the Spirit convicts us, He doesn't just show us the stain of sin—He offers the soap of grace. And when we respond, transformation begins.

A Clear Conscience

"How much more shall the blood of Christ… purge your conscience from dead works to serve the living God?" —Hebrews 9:14 (KJV)

One of the greatest gifts of conviction is the removal of guilt. When the Spirit reveals our sin, and we surrender, our conscience is cleansed.

You don't have to walk around feeling:

- Guilty
- Filthy
- Unworthy
- Ashamed

Conviction leads to confession, and confession opens the door to cleansing. When you repent, the weight lifts. The enemy's accusations lose their grip. You no longer hide—you walk in freedom.

> **"There is therefore now no condemnation to them which are in Christ Jesus…" —Romans 8:1 (KJV)**

If you're burdened by shame, don't run from conviction—run to it. It's not punishment—it's your path to peace.

A Renewed Spirit

> **"Create in me a clean heart, O God; and renew a right spirit within me." —Psalm 51:10 (KJV)**

Sin doesn't just dirty our hands—it drains our spirit. It makes us sluggish, cynical, and distant from God. But conviction breathes new life into what was once weary.

When we repent, the Spirit:

- Revives our hunger for prayer.
- Restores spiritual sensitivity.

Reigniting the Fire of Soul Winning in Our Churches

- Rekindles joy in worship.
- Realigns our desires with God's.

David, after his failure, didn't just want forgiveness—he wanted restoration. And the Spirit didn't shame him—He renewed him.

> **"Restore unto me the joy of thy salvation; and uphold me with thy free spirit." —Psalm 51:12 (KJV)**

Application

Don't settle for forgiveness alone—ask God for a renewed spirit and a fresh pursuit.

Joy Restored

> **"…thou shalt make me full of joy with thy countenance." —Acts 2:28 (KJV)**

Nothing kills joy like unrepented sin. But nothing restores joy like Spirit-led conviction and cleansing. Joy is not found in hiding—it's found in confession and restoration.

True joy returns when:

- We come clean before God.
- We receive His mercy fully.
- We stop performing and start abiding.

The enemy tells you your sin disqualifies you.
The Spirit says your surrender re-qualifies you.
That's the joy of salvation—the miracle of being made new.

> "Blessed is he whose transgression is forgiven, whose sin is covered." —Psalm 32:1 (KJV)

Peace Returning

> "Being justified by faith, we have peace with God through our Lord Jesus Christ." —Romans 5:1 (KJV)

Conviction doesn't leave you trembling—it leads you to tranquility. When the Spirit convicts and we respond, peace rushes in.

You no longer fear God's wrath—you walk in His embrace.
You no longer live in tension—you live in trust.
You no longer hide—you abide.
Conviction leads to peace with God and the peace of God.

> "And the peace of God, which passeth all understanding, shall keep your hearts and minds through Christ Jesus." —Philippians 4:7 (KJV)

If your heart is restless, ask yourself: Is the Spirit trying to cleanse something so that peace can return?

Conviction Is a Gift—Receive It

The church must stop treating conviction like it's harmful. It is one of the most loving acts of the Holy Spirit. He reveals, not to punish, but to restore. He uncovers, not to wound—but to heal.

When we welcome conviction:

- Hearts are softened.

- Altars are filled.
- Families are restored.
- Worship becomes pure.
- The fire of revival is ignited.

> **"Repent ye therefore, and be converted, that your sins may be blotted out, when the times of refreshing shall come…" —Acts 3:19 (KJV)**

There is no refreshing without repentance, and there is no repentance without conviction.

Let the Soap of Grace Cleanse the Stain of Sin

Jesus doesn't just point out the dirt—He bends down to wash it away.

The Spirit doesn't come to shame you—He comes to free you.
So don't resist conviction—run toward it.
Don't fear being exposed—celebrate being cleansed.
Don't carry the weight—release it.

Because when the Spirit convicts, He leaves you:

- Clear in conscience.
- Renewed in spirit.
- Restored in joy.
- Filled with peace.

> **"…though your sins be as scarlet, they shall be as white as snow." —Isaiah 1:18 (KJV)**

David was a murderer and adulterer. But when the Spirit convicted him, and he repented, he was made clean. And what followed was not shame—but worship.

> **"Purge me with hyssop, and I shall be clean: wash me, and I shall be whiter than snow." —Psalm 51:7 (KJV)**

What Happens When We Remove Conviction from the Church

When conviction is removed to make people "comfortable," we end up with:

- Crowds without conversion.
- Programs without power.
- Worship without wonder.
- Messages without movement.

People don't need flattery—they need freedom. And that freedom begins with conviction.

> **"They that are whole need not a physician; but they that are sick." —Luke 5:31 (KJV)**

The church must stop apologizing for conviction and instead thank God for it.

Welcome the Work of the Spirit

We need churches where people leave:

- Changed by the Word.

Reigniting the Fire of Soul Winning in Our Churches

- Challenged to grow.
- Chosen with purpose.
- Clean in heart.

Let us open the altar again—not just for prayer, but for purging. Let us welcome the weight of the Spirit again—not to push people down, but to raise them up.

> **"Search me, O God, and know my heart… and lead me in the way everlasting." —Psalm 139:23–24 (KJV)**

Let the Spirit convict.
Let the people weep.
Let the church become holy.
Let souls become new.

But when the Spirit is quenched:

- People attend church and remain in sin.
- Sermons become safe, not sanctifying.
- Altar calls disappear.
- Entertainment replaces encounter.

The absence of conviction is not a sign of success—it's a sign that the Spirit has been pushed to the back.

Application

If nobody's repenting, something's missing. The Spirit must be center stage, not backstage.

Let the Spirit Move Again

"...where the Spirit of the Lord is, there is liberty." —2 Corinthians 3:17 (KJV)

We cannot afford to run Spirit-less services. We cannot afford to host gatherings where God isn't invited. If we want revival, we must stop quenching and start yielding.

How Do We Quench the Spirit?

- Prioritizing control over surrender.
- Avoiding spiritual gifts out of fear or pride.
- Replacing prayer with programs.
- Ignoring conviction for crowd comfort.

How Do We Welcome Him Back?

- Pray: "Holy Spirit, You have full access."
- Teach and make room for spiritual gifts.
- Build altar time into every service.
- Yield leadership to His presence—even when it disrupts the schedule.

"Then the fire of the Lord fell..." —1 Kings 18:38 (KJV)

Let that be our testimony again. Let the Spirit be free. Let the fire return because a church that quenches the Spirit will die in dignity. But a church that welcomes Him will burn in glory.

"Not by might, nor by power, but by my spirit, saith the Lord..." —Zechariah 4:6 (KJV)

We don't need more structure—we need more surrender.

How to Stop Quenching the Spirit

- Allow the gifts of the Spirit to flow (see 1 Corinthians 12:7–11).
- Train leaders to recognize and respond to His prompting.
- Don't fear manifestations—discern them.
- Prioritize prayer, not programming, in service planning.

When the Spirit is honored, He brings power, direction, and breakthrough.

Cry Out for Fresh Baptism and Boldness: We Need Pentecost Again

"And they were all filled with the Holy Ghost..." —Acts 2:4 (KJV)

Pentecost was not just an event—it was the church's empowerment moment. And we need fresh Pentecosts again. Not historical reflection, but present outpouring.

You cannot fulfill a supernatural mission with natural strength. We must be baptized anew with fire.

Signs You Need a Fresh Baptism

- Fear overrides faith.
- Evangelism becomes rare.
- Prayer life is dry.
- Services lack power.

- Sin is tolerated instead of conquered.

"...be filled with the Spirit." —Ephesians 5:18 (KJV)

The baptism of the Holy Spirit doesn't just give you tongues—it gives you boldness, clarity, and unshakable witness.

How to Receive a Fresh Filling

- Ask—God gives to the hungry (see Luke 11:13).
- Repent of complacency.
- Spend time in prayer and worship without an agenda.
- Tarry until power comes (see Luke 24:49).

We don't need better personalities—we need burning people full of the Holy Ghost.

Allow the Spirit to Move Freely in Every Gathering – Let God Interrupt

"...then the house was filled with the cloud, even the house of the Lord..." —2 Chronicles 5:13–14 (KJV)

When was the last time God took over your service? When was the last time the agenda was interrupted by glory? A fire-filled church makes room for the Spirit—not just in language, but in reality.

In many modern gatherings:

- The schedule is sacred.
- The Spirit is silenced.
- The altar is rushed.

- The response is shallow.

We must make room again—for we cannot manufacture revival. We must host it.

How to Make Room for the Spirit

- Start services with prayer, not production.
- Wait on the Lord—don't rush worship or altar time.
- Allow tongues, prophecy, and healing to flow.
- Teach people how to discern the Spirit's leading.

"Let all things be done decently and in order." —1 Corinthians 14:40 (KJV)

But not without power. Let us choose Spirit-led order—not spiritless control.

Closing Challenge: Stir It Up

"…stir up the gift of God…" —2 Timothy 1:6 (KJV)

Fire doesn't rekindle itself. It must be pursued, stirred, and guarded. A fireless church cannot win a dying world.

Let every believer:

- Return to fasting and prayer.
- Preach and live with urgency.
- Honor the Holy Spirit.
- Cry out for fresh fire.

- Allow God to move without limits.

When we do, the church will not only burn again—it will blaze with revival power.

Cry Out for Fresh Baptism and Boldness – Seeking a New Infilling

> "...and they were all filled with the Holy Ghost... and they spake the word of God with boldness." —Acts 4:31 (KJV)

The church does not need more training before it needs more anointing. The early believers didn't rely on intellectual arguments—they were baptized with power, and they turned the world upside down.

The fire of soul winning is rekindled through fresh encounters with the Holy Spirit.

We must cry out for:

- A renewed infilling.
- A deeper hunger.
- A holy fire that burns fear, doubt, and timidity.

CHAPTER 18

CRY OUT FOR FRESH FIRE

> "…and they were all filled with the Holy Ghost, and they spake the word of God with boldness." —Acts 4:31 (KJV)

The fire of soul winning is not a learned technique—it is the result of an ongoing encounter with the Holy Spirit. The early church turned the world upside down, not because they were more educated or eloquent, but because they were filled with a supernatural fire that could not be quenched.

Today, the church needs more than good intentions—it needs a fresh baptism, a deeper hunger, and a holy boldness that sets fear on fire and turns timidity into testimony.

A Renewed Infilling – We Cannot Live on Yesterday's Flame

Many believers are living off a memory of the fire they once had. But the fire that once burned in them has become a flicker. The infilling of the Holy Spirit is not a one-time event—it is a continual necessity.

> "…be not drunk with wine… but be filled with the Spirit." —Ephesians 5:18 (KJV)

Reigniting the Fire of Soul Winning in Our Churches

There's a dangerous myth in the church: that a one-time encounter with God is enough to sustain a lifetime of spiritual fire. But we weren't called to live on memories—we were called to live in moment-by-moment dependence on the Holy Spirit.

The apostles were filled in Acts 2—but again in Acts 4. Why? Because fresh battles require fresh oil. New assignments demand new anointing. Yesterday's fire won't ignite today's lost souls.

The Command to Be Filled Is Ongoing

The Greek word for "be filled" in Ephesians 5:18 literally means, "be being filled." It's not a suggestion. It's a present, continuous command.

You don't fill a lamp once and forget it. If you don't refill it, it goes dark. And in a world growing darker by the hour, the church cannot afford to run on empty lamps.

Jesus described the wise virgins as those who kept oil in their lamps (see Matthew 25:1–13). In the same way, every believer and every church must make the fresh infilling of the Spirit a priority, not a luxury.

Why a Fresh Infilling Is Essential

1. **Without it, fear rules and boldness fades.**

    "Then Peter, filled with the Holy Ghost, said unto them…" —Acts 4:8 (KJV)

Peter was once afraid to even admit he knew Jesus. But after the upper room, he stood before crowds and rulers with boldness and power.

The difference? A fresh infilling.

When the Spirit fills a person:

- Fear breaks.
- Courage rises.
- Boldness flows.
- Obedience overtakes hesitation.

A church without a fresh infilling will stay silent when it should speak, hide when it should shine, and compromise when it should confront.

> **"For God hath not given us the spirit of fear..." —2 Timothy 1:7 (KJV)**

2. Without it, evangelism becomes duty, not desire.

> **"...woe is unto me, if I preach not the gospel!" —1 Corinthians 9:16 (KJV)**

Evangelism birthed in duty will eventually die in discouragement. But evangelism birthed in the Spirit is fueled by fire.

When you're freshly filled with the Holy Ghost:

- You don't need to be begged to witness.

- The lost become your priority, not a project.
- Your heart burns with urgency for their eternity.

A Spirit-filled believer doesn't evangelize because they "have to"—they evangelize because they can't help it.

> **"…and they were all filled with the Holy Ghost… and they spake the word of God with boldness." —Acts 4:31 (KJV)**

3. Without it, spiritual gifts go dormant.

> **"Neglect not the gift that is in thee…" —1 Timothy 4:14 (KJV)**

The gifts of the Spirit are not decorations—they're tools for the harvest. But without a fresh infilling, those tools go unused.

Tongues grow quiet. Prophecy ceases. Words of knowledge dry up. Healing prayers stop. Why? Not because God left—but because we stopped seeking.

Fresh infilling awakens:

- Discernment
- Revelation
- Intercession
- Authority

The church becomes alive in the supernatural again, not just in doctrine, but in demonstration.

4. **Without it, the church becomes powerless.**

> "Having a form of godliness, but denying the power thereof…" —2 Timothy 3:5 (KJV)

A church without fresh oil may look organized, but it will lack anointing. It may attract crowds, but it won't make disciples. It may run events, but it won't birth movements.

— No Spirit = No Power.
— No Power = No Fire.
— No Fire = No Fruit.

It's not enough to talk about Pentecost—we must live it.

> "Not by might, nor by power, but by my Spirit, saith the Lord." —Zechariah 4:6 (KJV)

A powerless church cannot confront a powerful enemy. But a freshly filled church walks in victory.

How to Seek a Fresh Infilling

- **Ask and Expect**

  > "…how much more shall your heavenly Father give the Holy Spirit to them that ask him?" —Luke 11:13 (KJV).

- **Repent of Complacency**

> **"Create in me a clean heart, O God; and renew a right spirit within me."** —Psalm 51:10 (KJV)

- **Tarry in His Presence**

> **"But they that wait upon the Lord shall renew their strength…"** —Isaiah 40:31 (KJV)

- **Surrender Your Will**

The fire falls on sacrifice. Lay your plans down and invite Him to take over.

Don't Live on Yesterday's Fire

Your last encounter was powerful—but it's not enough. Your last infilling was real—but you need more.

Cry out again.
Surrender again.
Wait again.
And watch the fire fall again.

> **"The fire shall ever be burning upon the altar; it shall never go out."** —Leviticus 6:13 (KJV)

Let the oil flow. Let the fire burn. Let the church be filled again.

> **"Then laid they their hands on them, and they received the Holy Ghost."** —Acts 8:17 (KJV)

Just as the apostles were repeatedly filled (Acts 2 and Acts 4), we too must cry out for fresh fire—not just to speak in tongues, but to walk in power.

A Deeper Hunger – The Fire Falls on the Desperate

> **"Blessed are they which do hunger and thirst after righteousness: for they shall be filled." —Matthew 5:6 (KJV)**

Hunger is the currency of heaven. God responds to desperation more than presentation. He fills the hungry—not the curious.

The church must develop a spiritual appetite for the fire of God again—not entertainment, not comfort, not casual Christianity.

How to cultivate holy hunger:

- Fast regularly to weaken the flesh and stir the spirit.
- Pray dangerously: *"God, take everything that quenches You."*
- Remove distractions and idols.
- Linger in God's presence—don't rush prayer.

> **"I stretch forth my hands unto thee: my soul thirsteth after thee, as a thirsty land. Selah." —Psalm 143:6 (KJV)**

Hungry people are bold people. When you're full of Him, fear has no room to live.

Holy Fire Burns Fear, Doubt, and Timidity

> "For God hath not given us the spirit of fear; but of power, and of love, and of a sound mind." —2 Timothy 1:7 (KJV)

Fear is one of the greatest enemies of evangelism. It whispers:

- "What if they reject you?"
- "What if you don't know what to say?"
- "What if you fail?"

But the fire of the Holy Spirit doesn't negotiate with fear—it consumes it.

> "But ye shall receive power, after that the Holy Ghost is come upon you: and ye shall be witnesses…" —Acts 1:8 (KJV)

The evidence of Spirit baptism is more than tongues—it's boldness for witness. It's courage to speak up. It's a burden that outweighs fear.

When the fire breaks chains:

- Fear becomes faith.
- Doubt becomes declaration.
- Timidity becomes testimony.

Like Peter, who denied Christ out of fear but stood boldly at Pentecost, we too must go from silence to shouting the gospel.

Pastor Dr. Claudine Benjamin

A Church on Fire Cannot Be Silent

> **"And when they had prayed, the place was shaken… and they were all filled with the Holy Ghost, and they spake the word of God with boldness." —Acts 4:31 (KJV)**

Silence is not the mark of a burning church. A church truly ablaze with the Holy Spirit is impossible to ignore. It shakes cities, fills altars, and awakens the spiritually dead. It doesn't simply gather—it goes. It doesn't merely talk—it testifies.

In today's climate of cultural compromise and spiritual apathy, the church must not be polite when God is calling for power. A Spirit-filled, Spirit-led church doesn't shrink back—it stands up. It cries out. It reaches out. And it never stops burning.

A Church on Fire Cries Out for Fresh Baptism

> **"And be not drunk with wine… but be filled with the Spirit." —Ephesians 5:18 (KJV)**

The first mark of a burning church is its desperation for God. The Spirit-filled church is never satisfied with yesterday's encounters—it is always crying out for more.

When the fire burns:

- Prayer meetings become upper rooms.
- Worship turns into warfare.
- Hunger intensifies until heaven responds.

Reigniting the Fire of Soul Winning in Our Churches

The early church prayed constantly for fresh power, and the result was undeniable.

> **"And they were all filled with the Holy Ghost… and the same day there were added unto them about three thousand souls."** —Acts 2:4, 41 (KJV)

We must reject stagnant Christianity and cry out again for:

- A fresh baptism of power.
- A fresh outpouring of boldness.
- A fresh awakening of spiritual gifts.
- A fresh compassion for the lost.

Revival never comes to the satisfied—it comes to the desperate.

A Church on Fire Refuses to Live on Stale Fire

> **"The fire shall ever be burning upon the altar; it shall never go out."** —Leviticus 6:13 (KJV)

Stale fire is smoke with no flame. It's spiritual memory without present intensity. Many churches today live off of past revivals and old testimonies, but a church that refuses to live on stale fire keeps its altar burning daily.

Signs of stale fire:

- No passion in worship.
- No hunger in the preaching.
- No repentance at the altar.

- No signs, wonders, or salvations.

Fresh fire demands fresh surrender.
Fresh fire requires daily sacrifice.
Fresh fire means refusing to pretend when the flame has gone out.

Let the church return to the altar—not as a formality, but as a furnace of transformation.

A Church on Fire Hungers for More of God

"Blessed are they which do hunger and thirst after righteousness: for they shall be filled." —Matthew 5:6 (KJV)

A Spirit-filled church is a hungry church. It doesn't hunger for performance, platforms, or recognition—it hungers for the presence and power of God.

This hunger shows itself in:

- Persistent prayer.
- Deep intercession.
- Intimate worship.
- Willing sacrifice.

This is not emotional hype—it's a holy pursuit.

When Moses encountered the burning bush, he turned aside. That fire led him into divine destiny (see Exodus 3). So too, a hungry church will pause everything else to chase the flame.

A Church on Fire Stands Unashamed in Public Witness

> "For I am not ashamed of the gospel of Christ: for it is the power of God unto salvation..." —Romans 1:16 (KJV)

The fire of the Holy Spirit doesn't just move in private—it manifests in public.

A Spirit-filled, Spirit-led church doesn't whisper the gospel—it declares it boldly. It's not intimidated by politics, culture, or persecution. It knows that souls are at stake and that silence is not an option.

A witnessing church:

- Preaches on the street and in the sanctuary.
- Testifies in homes, offices, and schools.
- Isn't afraid to be labeled or rejected.
- Burns with urgency and clarity.

Peter preached, and 3,000 were saved (see Acts 2). Stephen testified, and heaven opened (see Acts 7). Paul evangelized until empires were shaken. None of them was ashamed—and neither should we be.

Break the Silence—Let the Fire Speak

Silence is comfortable, but fire is confrontational. When the church burns again:

- Prayer will roar.
- Preaching will convict.
- Witnesses will rise.
- Revival will break out.

We do not need better branding. We are in need of burning. Let us cry out. Let us burn again. Let us become the church that cannot be silent.

> **"But his word was in mine heart as a burning fire shut up in my bones." —Jeremiah 20:9 (KJV)**

The world is watching. Hell is raging. Heaven is ready. Let the church burn—and let it speak.

> **"My heart was hot within me... then spake I with my tongue." —Psalm 39:3 (KJV)**

When the fire is real, it cannot be hidden. It must be shared. Preached. Demonstrated. Released.

Cry Out Until the Fire Falls Again

- Cry out in prayer.
- Cry out in worship.
- Cry out in fasting.
- Cry out for your city.
- Cry out for your church.
- Cry out for your calling.

Reigniting the Fire of Soul Winning in Our Churches

Because the fire of soul winning isn't stirred by performance—it's ignited by encounter.

> **"And there appeared unto them cloven tongues like as of fire... and they were all filled..." —Acts 2:3–4 (KJV)**

Don't Settle for Smoke—Seek the Flame

> **"Blow the trumpet in Zion, sanctify a fast, call a solemn assembly... Let the priests, the ministers of the Lord, weep between the porch and the altar." —Joel 2:15–17 (KJV)**

Throughout scripture and church history, one sound has always preceded revival: a cry. Not a whisper of convenience, but a desperate, urgent, unrelenting cry for God's fire to fall again.

The church today doesn't need more activity—it needs more agony.
Not better systems, but brokenness.
Not more ideas, but intercession.

When the church cries out, heaven responds. When we break, God breaks in.

Let the Church Cry Out Until Altar Calls Overflow

> **"And when they heard this, they were pricked in their heart, and said... What shall we do?" —Acts 2:37 (KJV)**

When the church truly burns with the fire of God, altar calls are not a ritual—they are a rescue. People come weeping, surrendering, repenting—not because they're emotionally stirred, but spiritually awakened.

We must cry out until:

- Altar moments cannot be rushed.
- The lost run to the altar before the invitation.
- There is groaning and travailing at the front, not just music.

A cold altar reflects a cold church. But a church that cries out will soon have altars that overflow.

Let the Church Cry Out Until the Timid Become Messengers

> **"Then Peter, filled with the Holy Ghost, said unto them…"** —Acts 4:8 (KJV)

Peter went from denying Jesus to declaring Him, because he was filled with fire. The timid are transformed in the place of prayer. Weakness turns to witness when the Spirit comes upon a person.

We must cry out until:

- Fear is burned out of our pulpits.
- Silence is replaced with a bold declaration.
- Every day believers become fearless evangelists.

> **"Ye shall receive power… and ye shall be witnesses…"** —Acts 1:8 (KJV)

When the church cries out, timidity is broken, and the gospel is preached without shame.

Let the Church Cry Out Until the Lost Are Saved in Every Service

> **"And the Lord added to the church daily such as should be saved." —Acts 2:47 (KJV)**

The mark of a church in revival is not just deeper teaching—it's daily salvation. Souls saved—not occasionally, but continually. Because a burning church draws the broken, and a gospel-centered church rescues the lost.

We must cry out until:

- Every message points to the cross.
- Every gathering calls for repentance.
- Every member becomes a soul-winner.

The harvest is waiting. The fire is ready. But the church must cry out until heaven rains salvation again.

Let the Church Cry Out Until the Streets Are Filled with Witnesses

> **"…they that were scattered abroad went every where preaching the word." —Acts 8:4 (KJV)**

In the early church, evangelism didn't just happen inside buildings—it happened in the streets, homes, markets, and prisons. Every believer was a flame—spreading fire wherever they went.

We must cry out until:

- Evangelism moves from events to lifestyle.
- Prayer meetings overflow into neighborhoods.
- Teenagers preach in schools.
- Co-workers become converts.

Let us not be content with packed pews—we want flooded streets full of witnesses.

Let the Church Cry Out Until the Fire Burns Again in Our Gatherings

> **"And when the day of Pentecost was fully come... there came a sound from heaven as of a rushing mighty wind..." —Acts 2:1–2 (KJV)**

We've had well-run services—but have we had Spirit-filled ones? Have we had order—but no outpouring? Precision without presence? It's time for fire again—not figuratively, but literally. The tangible, unmistakable, consuming fire of God.

We must cry out until:

- Our gatherings are marked by glory.
- Tongues, prophecy, healing, and conviction manifest freely.
- We stay at the altar long after the benediction.
- Fire burns in every heart, every home, every hall.

When fire falls, everything changes.

Don't Stop Until It Falls

> **"They continued with one accord in prayer and supplication…"** —Acts 1:14 (KJV)

They cried out—and the fire came.
They waited—and heaven responded.
They wept—and were filled.

Let us cry out again:

- For our cities.
- For our children.
- For our pulpits.
- For our prodigals.
- For a fresh baptism of power.

Cry out until it falls.

> **"Then the fire of the Lord fell, and consumed the burnt sacrifice…"** —1 Kings 18:38 (KJV)

Let the Church Cry Out, and Let the Fire Fall Again

> **"…be filled with the Spirit."** —Ephesians 5:18 (KJV)

The same Peter who denied Christ became the fiery preacher of Pentecost. What changed? The Spirit came upon him.

We too need to be filled again—and again. Not with religion. Not with routine. But with fire from on high.

Allow the Spirit to Move Freely in Every Gathering – Cultivating a Spirit-Led Atmosphere

> **"Now the Lord is that Spirit…"** **—2 Corinthians 3:17 (KJV)**

The Holy Spirit is not a guest—we are His guests. And when we yield to Him, fire falls. When we schedule Him out, heaven stays silent.

In many churches:

- Services are rushed.
- Altars are empty.
- Prayer is minimal.
- Control replaces flow.

But a Spirit-filled church gives space for:

- Tongues and interpretation.
- Healing and deliverance.
- Prophetic words.

Make Room for the Spirit – Hosting the Fire, Not Containing It

> **"…the house was filled with the cloud, even the house of the Lord… for the glory of the Lord had filled the house of God."** **—2 Chronicles 5:13–14 (KJV)**

In the upper room, the disciples didn't host a service—they hosted the Spirit. They weren't looking for a moment; they were waiting for a manifestation. And when the Holy Spirit came, He came with fire.

Today, too many churches have carefully crafted atmospheres but no abiding presence. The order of service is tight, the transitions are smooth, but the altars are cold. Why? Because the Holy Spirit is no longer leading. He is being managed.

We must stop inviting Him as a guest and start yielding to Him as the Owner.

When We Schedule Him Out, Heaven Stays Silent

> "Ichabod... The glory is departed from Israel." —1 Samuel 4:21 (KJV)

It's possible to have church without God. The music can move people. The preaching can inspire. The crowd can be large. But if the Holy Spirit isn't moving, we're hosting an event—not an encounter.

When churches rush, restrict, or resist the Spirit, we:

- Lose our power.
- Forfeit true transformation.
- Silence conviction.
- Quench revival before it begins.

The result? Churches that are:

- Loud but powerless.
- Active but fruitless.
- Impressive but empty.

The Signs of a Fireless Church

- **Services Are Rushed**

"could ye not watch with me one hour?" —Matthew 26:40 (KJV)

We prioritize time limits over divine timing. We move when the clock says move, not when the Spirit says stay.

- **Altars Are Empty**

No conviction. No repentance. No hunger. When the Spirit isn't welcome, people aren't drawn to surrender.

- **Prayer Is Minimal**

Prayer is pushed aside for announcements, transitions, and tight programming. Yet, it is prayer that births power.

- **Control Replaces Flow**

The Spirit is edited for safety. Leadership holds the reins so tightly, there's no room for divine interruption.

"The wind bloweth where it listeth…" —John 3:8 (KJV)

Reigniting the Fire of Soul Winning in Our Churches

The Spirit doesn't fit into schedules. He moves where He's free to move.

What a Spirit-Filled Church Looks Like

> **"Let all things be done decently and in order." —1 Corinthians 14:40 (KJV)**

Order doesn't mean absence of power. A Spirit-filled church is not chaotic—it's led. It moves with the Spirit, not in spite of Him.

Tongues and Interpretation Are Present

> **"If any man speak in an unknown tongue… let one interpret." —1 Corinthians 14:27 (KJV)**

The gifts of the Spirit aren't meant to be silenced. They're meant to edify the body. Churches that host the Spirit give room for:

- Tongues
- Interpretation
- Prophetic confirmation
- Holy awe

This isn't outdated—it's New Testament.

Healing and Deliverance Flow Freely

> **"And these signs shall follow them that believe… they shall lay hands on the sick, and they shall recover." —Mark 16:17–18**

When the Spirit moves, sickness is healed, demons flee, and chains break. But this can't happen when altar time is cut short or prayer teams are untrained and unavailable.

Spirit-filled churches:

- Expect miracles.
- Provide room for deliverance.
- Equip saints to minister in power.

Prophetic Words Are Honored

> **"Despise not prophesyings." —1 Thessalonians 5:20 (KJV)**

God still speaks. And He speaks to edify, exhort, and comfort (see 1 Corinthians 14:3). In many churches, prophetic utterances are suppressed due to fear of emotionalism or error. But when the Spirit leads, prophetic voices are:

- Verified
- Accountable
- Anointed
- Fruitful

We need prophetic direction—not just programmed content.

Altar Encounters Outlast the Benediction

> **"The fire shall ever be burning upon the altar; it shall never go out." —Leviticus 6:13 (KJV)**

Reigniting the Fire of Soul Winning in Our Churches

Altar moments are where the fire lands:

- Sins are confessed.
- Callings are birthed.
- Tears water the next revival.
- Souls meet Jesus.

A Spirit-filled church doesn't rush the altar. It honors the moment. It waits. It ministers. It watches people linger until they're changed.

How to Restore Room for the Spirit

- Train your team to follow the Spirit, not the schedule.
- Allow extra time for altar response, healing, and deliverance.
- Teach on the gifts of the Spirit—not just in theory, but in practice.
- Open the door for the prophetic and intercessory flow.
- Embrace extended services when the presence is thick.

"...tarry ye... until ye be endued with power from on high." —Luke 24:49 (KJV)

If you want Pentecost power, you must be willing to wait for it.

Host Him, Don't Hinder Him

A Spirit-filled church is not known by what it can produce, but by Whom it can host. Let the music play longer. Let the preaching stay weighty. Let the altar remain open. Let the schedule bend to the wind of the Spirit.

Let fire fall again—not because we planned it, but because we made room for it.

> "...and the Lord, whom ye seek, shall suddenly come to his temple..." —Malachi 3:1 (KJV)

Prepare the room. He will come where the Spirit is honored.

Make Room for the Spirit – Let Heaven Interrupt Again

> "Now the Lord is that Spirit: and where the Spirit of the Lord is, there is liberty." —2 Corinthians 3:17 (KJV)

The Holy Spirit is not an honored guest in the church—He is the Lord of the church. We don't host Him—we are hosted by Him. But in many modern churches, His presence has been pushed to the margins in favor of tight schedules, professional polish, and crowd-friendly services.

We say, *"Come, Holy Spirit,"* but we leave Him no time, no space, and no control.

When the Spirit Is Scheduled Out, Heaven Stays Silent

Church services today are often:

- Rushed to fit into cultural expectations.
- Measured by transitions, not transformation.
- Focused on excellence rather than encounter.

> "...and limited the Holy One of Israel." —Psalm 78:41 (KJV)

We limit God not because He lacks power, but because we refuse to yield.

Where there is no room for the Spirit, there is:

- No revival.
- No repentance.
- No deliverance.
- No fire.

And, most dangerously, no glory.

Symptoms of a Spirit-Suppressed Church

> "Having a form of godliness, but denying the power thereof." —2 Timothy 3:5 (KJV)

- Services are rushed
- Worship is clocked.
- Sermons are timed.
- Altars are skipped.
- Altars are empty.
- There's no expectation for brokenness.
- The Spirit is not invited to minister deeply.
- Conviction is replaced by comfort.
- Prayer is minimal
- Meetings open and close in routine prayer.
- Intercession is rare.

- Fasting is forgotten.
- Control replaces flow.
- Leadership micromanages the Spirit's movement.
- Everything must fit a script.
- Spontaneous obedience is viewed as disorder.

This is not New Testament church. This is institutional Christianity without Pentecost.

What Happens When We Make Room for the Spirit

When the church yields, God takes over. And when He takes over, everything changes.

> **"And suddenly there came a sound from heaven… and there appeared unto them cloven tongues like as of fire…" —Acts 2:2–3 (KJV)**

A yielded church is marked by:

1. **Tongues and interpretation.**

    > **"I would that ye all spake with tongues… if there be no interpreter, let him keep silence…" —1 Corinthians 14:5, 28 (KJV)**

Tongues are not a distraction—they're a demonstration. When properly practiced, they edify the body and confirm the presence of God.

A Spirit-filled church:

- Doesn't silence tongues.
- Teaches and discerns their operation.
- Welcomes interpretation for the strengthening of the saints.

2. Healing and deliverance.

> **"These signs shall follow them that believe… they shall lay hands on the sick, and they shall recover." —Mark 16:17–18 (KJV)**

The early church saw miracles in homes, streets, and gatherings. So should we.

Healing is not confined to revival nights—it belongs in every atmosphere where the Spirit is welcomed. When He moves, sickness leaves, chains break, and demons flee.

> **"But if I cast out devils by the Spirit of God, then the kingdom of God is come unto you." —Matthew 12:28 (KJV)**

3. Prophetic words.

> **"He that prophesieth speaketh unto men to edification, and exhortation, and comfort." —1 Corinthians 14:3 (KJV)**

Where the Spirit is free, the prophetic voice is restored—not to predict entertainment, but to:

- Warn
- Build up

- Confirm
- Reveal direction

A Spirit-yielded church doesn't chase the prophetic—it hosts it properly, with testing, order, and discernment.

4. Altar encounters that last beyond the benediction.

> **"So that the priests could not stand to minister by reason of the cloud: for the glory of the Lord had filled the house of God." —2 Chronicles 5:14 (KJV)**

True altars do not operate on timers. They are eternal moments where heaven touches earth. In many churches, altar time has been reduced to mere symbolism—but in the Bible, altars were:

- Places of fire.
- Places of sacrifice.
- Places of calling.
- Places of transformation.

In a Spirit-led atmosphere:

- People linger.
- Lives are changed.
- Weeping turns to joy.
- Silence is broken by the sound of glory.

These moments can't be scripted—they must be surrendered to.

A church that makes room for the Spirit:

- Waits for His presence, even when it disrupts the plan.
- Teaches the gifts and expects them to operate.
- Builds services around God's will, not man's convenience.
- Prioritizes presence over presentation.
- Yields fully, even if it costs comfort, control, or reputation.

Let Heaven Interrupt Again

> **"He that hath an ear, let him hear what the Spirit saith unto the churches..." —Revelation 2:7 (KJV)**

We must let God speak again. Move again. Heal again. Fill again. Not in a back room, not under restriction—but in the center of every gathering.

When the Spirit is allowed to move, the lost will be saved, the bound will be loosed, and the fire will return to the altar.

Church, make room. Heaven is waiting to interrupt our plans—with revival.

> **"So that the priests could not stand to minister by reason of the cloud: for the glory of the Lord had filled the house of God." —2 Chronicles 5:14 (KJV)**

That's what happens when the Spirit moves freely—human plans are laid down, and God takes over.

The Challenge

The fire doesn't rekindle itself. It must be stirred.

- Through fasting, we humble ourselves.
- Through urgent preaching, we awaken others.
- Through yielding, we invite the Holy Spirit back to His rightful place.
- Through crying out, we are filled anew.
- Through freedom, God reigns in our gatherings.

Let the church no longer settle for imitation fire. Let us pay the price for the real flame.

> **"The fire shall ever be burning upon the altar; it shall never go out." —Leviticus 6:13 (KJV)**

Fire for the Mission

You cannot reach the lost with lukewarmness. The world isn't changed by coolness—it's changed by fire. What Pentecost released is still available. And it's needed now more than ever.

> **"…fervent in spirit; serving the Lord." —Romans 12:11 (KJV)**

The fire doesn't come to entertain—it comes to empower.

Church, return to the fire. Your mission depends on it.

CHAPTER 19

REJECTING SHOWMANSHIP – RETURNING TO AUTHENTIC POWER

> "Having a form of godliness, but denying the power thereof: from such turn away." —2 Timothy 3:5 (KJV)

The modern church has become masterful at creating experiences—yet in many places, it has lost encounter. We've learned to craft atmospheres, produce polished services, and impress people with creativity—but too often, we've traded presence for performance, and power for personality.

God is calling His church to reject showmanship and return to authentic power.

The Danger of Religious Performance

Showmanship:

- Exalts talent over truth.
- Prioritizes emotions over transformation.
- Draws crowds but doesn't make disciples.
- Avoids conviction to maintain comfort.

> "For they loved the praise of men more than the praise of God." —John 12:43 (KJV)

A church that seeks applause more than repentance has lost its way. God's glory will not rest on performance—it rests on purity, prayer, and preaching.

Return to the Power Source

The early church didn't have what we have today—yet they had what we desperately need:

- Boldness that spoke up in the face of fear.
- Miracles that confirmed the message.
- Conviction that led to repentance.
- Salvations that multiplied the kingdom.
- Apostolic authority that governed regions in the Spirit.

Boldness That Spoke Up in the Face of Fear

The early church was not merely enthusiastic—it was fearless. In the face of persecution, imprisonment, and even death, they refused to be silent. Boldness was not arrogance—it was anointed courage fueled by the Holy Spirit.

Peter and John stood before religious leaders and declared: **"…we cannot but speak the things which we have seen and heard." (Acts 4:20 - KJV).**

Their boldness was contagious and confrontational. It didn't ask permission. It didn't bow to political pressure. It wasn't afraid of public backlash. It was birthed in prayer and confirmed by power.

How boldness looks today:

- Speaking the truth in a culture of compromise.
- Preaching repentance when others preach comfort.
- Refusing to water down the gospel for popularity.
- Standing for righteousness in hostile environments.

> **"The wicked flee when no man pursueth: but the righteous are bold as a lion." —Proverbs 28:1 (KJV)**

The modern church must reclaim this kind of boldness, not for controversy, but for commission.

Miracles That Confirmed the Message

> **"And by the hands of the apostles were many signs and wonders wrought among the people." —Acts 5:12a (KJV)**

The early church didn't just preach about power—they walked in it. Miracles were not rare; they were expected. They didn't replace the gospel—they confirmed it.

> **"And they went forth... the Lord working with them, and confirming the word with signs following." —Mark 16:20 (KJV)**

From healing the lame (see Acts 3) to raising the dead (see Acts 9), miracles were the natural result of supernatural obedience.

Today's church must recover:

- A hunger for healing.
- A faith for deliverance.
- A trust in the Spirit to demonstrate the kingdom.
- A refusal to settle for powerless ministry.

We cannot explain away what we are supposed to walk in. The message is powerful, but it's meant to be accompanied by signs.

Conviction That Led to Repentance

"Now when they heard this, they were pricked in their heart, and said… What shall we do?" —Acts 2:37 (KJV)

The preaching of the early church was not about comfort—it was about conviction. Peter's sermon at Pentecost cut through the crowd. It didn't flatter. It exposed sin and pointed to the cross.

Conviction is the work of the Holy Spirit. It doesn't condemn—it awakens. It drives us to cry out for change. And in the early church, conviction was common.

What conviction produces:

- Weeping at the altar.
- Public repentance.
- Holiness among the saints.
- A deep awareness of eternity.

"…he will reprove the world of sin, and of righteousness, and of judgment." —John 16:8 (KJV)

When we preach with truth and power, hearts are pierced, and souls are saved. The church today must stop apologizing for conviction—it's how God rescues the lost.

Salvations That Multiplied the Kingdom

"Then they that gladly received his word were baptized: and the same day there were added unto them about three thousand souls." —Acts 2:41 (KJV)

The early church was explosive in growth, not because of strategy, but because of Spirit-led obedience. Souls were saved by the thousands. And it wasn't just a moment of decision—it was a movement of transformation.

Every sermon, every miracle, every act of boldness pointed to one goal: harvesting souls for the kingdom.

What real salvation looks like:

- Hearts turned toward Christ.
- Lives radically changed.
- Entire households saved (see Acts 16:31).
- Baptisms without delay (see Acts 8:36–38).

"…the Lord added to the church daily such as should be saved." —Acts 2:47 (KJV)

We don't need better church marketing—we need a burden for souls. The early church wasn't just growing—it was multiplying, because salvation was central.

Apostolic Authority That Governed Regions in the Spirit

> "...with great power gave the apostles witness of the resurrection... and great grace was upon them all." — Acts 4:33 (KJV)

The apostles weren't just teachers—they were territorial leaders in the Spirit. They governed cities not with political clout, but with heavenly authority. Their presence brought disruption to systems, healing to communities, and order to the body of Christ.

What apostolic authority looks like today:

- Planting churches in unreached areas.
- Casting down strongholds (2 Corinthians 10:4).
- Raising up leaders and multiplying laborers.
- Challenging false doctrine and spiritual darkness.

> "Truly the signs of an apostle were wrought among you in all patience, in signs, and wonders, and mighty deeds." —2 Corinthians 12:12 (KJV)

Apostolic authority isn't about a title—it's about governing with fire and faith. Today's church must move from celebrity to commissioning, from hierarchy to Holy Ghost authority.

The power is still available. The harvest is still ready. The question is—will we return to what works?

The fire of soul winning flowed through the early church because they had power from on high.

Let us not envy their results without embracing their cost. Let us not admire their miracles if we won't pursue their devotion.

> **"But ye shall receive power, after that the Holy Ghost is come upon you: and ye shall be witnesses..." —Acts 1:8 (KJV)**

Church, the early fire is still available—if we'll return to the altar where it began.

> **"And with great power gave the apostles witness of the resurrection... and great grace was upon them all." — Acts 4:33 (KJV)**

They didn't aim to be impressive—they aimed to be effective.

God Is Not Looking for Performers

He's looking for:

- Intercessors.
- Preachers who will speak the truth in love.
- Worshipers who sing from a place of brokenness.
- Churches that welcome the Holy Spirit, not silence Him.

God will not anoint what we perform. He anoints what we surrender.

People God Anoints: Profiles of Surrendered Vessels

1. The Intercessor – Heaven's Secret Weapon

> "And I sought for a man among them, that should make up the hedge, and stand in the gap before me for the land…" —Ezekiel 22:30 (KJV)

The intercessor is not seen on stages, but felt in the Spirit. This person labors in prayer when no one else is watching. Their burden births revival. Their prayers prepare the soil for soul winning. They aren't driven by spotlight, but by spiritual assignment.

Traits

- Weeps for the lost.
- Prays until something breaks.
- Feels God's heart deeply.
- Knows how to war in the Spirit.

Modern Example

That grandmother in the back pew whose knees are worn but whose prayers shake hell.

Challenge

You don't need a platform to change lives: just a burden, a closet, and a cry.

2. **The Truth-Telling Preacher – Uncompromised in the Pulpit**

   > "Preach the word; be instant in season, out of season… reprove, rebuke, exhort…" —2 Timothy 4:2 (KJV)

God is not looking for charismatic communicators—He is raising up convictional voices. This preacher doesn't dilute the gospel. They don't avoid tough truths. They don't preach for applause—they preach for repentance.

Traits

- Filled with the Word and fire.
- Speaks truth with compassion.
- Confronts compromise.
- Carries a prophetic edge.

Biblical Model

John the Baptist—crying out in the wilderness, preparing the way of the Lord (see Luke 3:4–6).

Challenge

Will you speak what God says, even if it costs your platform?

3. **The Broken Worshiper – Pure Before Powerful**

   "The sacrifices of God are a broken spirit: a broken and a contrite heart…" —Psalm 51:17 (KJV)

This worshiper doesn't sing for show—they sing from the deep wells of experience with God. Their voice may be beautiful, but their anointing is birthed in tears. They've been crushed—and now carry a sound that pierces hearts.

Traits

- Leads worship from personal surrender.
- Ushers in God's presence, not just emotion.
- Values presence over performance.
- Has oil that came through pressing.

Biblical Model

Mary of Bethany—who broke her alabaster box and poured it at Jesus' feet (see Luke 7:37–38).

Challenge

Your worship is most powerful when it flows from the ashes of your altar.

4. The Spirit-Welcoming Church – A Place Where Fire Falls

"Quench not the Spirit." —1 Thessalonians 5:19 (KJV)

This isn't a person—it's a body; a church that isn't obsessed with order over outpouring; a church that tears up the schedule when heaven speaks; a church where tongues flow, prophecy is honored, and sinners are weeping at the altar—a resting place for revival.

Traits

- Makes room for God to move freely.
- Builds the service around presence, not preference.
- Honors spiritual gifts and teaches them biblically.
- Doesn't apologize for fire—it expects it.

Modern Picture

Not the biggest church in town—but the one where people walk in and say, "Surely, God is in this place."

Challenge

Is your church a sanctuary for the Spirit—or a stage for performance?

5. The Surrendered Vessel – The One God Anoints

"But the Lord said unto Samuel, Look not on his countenance, or on the height of his stature... for the Lord looketh on the heart." —1 Samuel 16:7 (KJV)

This person doesn't check all the boxes on man's resume—but God says, "That's the one I'll use." They may be young, overlooked, imperfect, or unknown—but they are surrendered. And God always anoints surrender.

Traits

- Doesn't strive for status.
- Lives crucified to self.
- Obeys quickly.
- Desires God's glory above their own gain.

Biblical Model

David—the shepherd boy who didn't look the part but had a heart after God (see 1 Samuel 13:14).

Challenge

God won't anoint what you perform. But He will set fire to what you surrender.

Performers May Impress—But Only the Surrendered Carry Fire

You can rehearse your craft.
You can perfect your presentation.
You can grow your crowd.
But if you're not yielded, you're just performing.

> **"Not by might, nor by power, but by my Spirit…" — Zechariah 4:6 (KJV)**

God is still looking for people who tremble at His Word, burn for His name, and carry His gospel—not for applause, but for impact.

> **"…the anointing… abideth in you, and ye need not that any man teach you…" —1 John 2:27 (KJV)**

CHAPTER 20

A CALL TO RETURN

Let the church turn down the lights if it must, but turn up the Word. Let us move away from manipulation and back to ministry. Let us reject showmanship—and seek the Spirit once again.

Rekindling the Burden for Souls

> "Mine eye affecteth mine heart…" —Lamentations 3:51 (KJV)

The fire of soul winning starts with burden. Before we preach, before we witness, before we go—we must feel. Without a burden, outreach becomes an obligation. Without compassion, the great commission becomes a lifeless command.

Too many in the church today have grown numb. We sing, serve, and even lead, but we don't weep for the lost anymore.

The Problem Isn't Willingness—It's Brokenness

We've taught evangelism methods. We've run outreach events. But what we desperately need is a broken heart.

> "But when he saw the multitudes, he was moved with compassion on them…" —Matthew 9:36 (KJV)

Jesus didn't start with strategy—He started with sight. He saw people clearly. He saw their need. He saw their spiritual condition. And His heart broke.

What Happens When the Burden Is Gone?

- Evangelism becomes rare.
- Altars stay empty.
- Outreach is forced, not fueled.
- Comfort replaces calling.
- Souls are no longer the focus—church culture is.

"Woe to them that are at ease in Zion…" —Amos 6:1 (KJV)

When the church loses its tears, it loses its fire.

How to Rekindle the Burden

- Pray dangerously – "Lord, break my heart for what breaks Yours."
- Visit broken places – Go where pain is visible: prisons, shelters, hospitals.
- Fast for compassion – Fasting softens the heart and clarifies vision.
- Remember your own rescue – Recall where God brought you from.

"Restore unto me the joy of thy salvation… then will I teach transgressors thy ways…" —Psalm 51:12–13 (KJV)

Burden leads to boldness. Burden fuels consistency. Burden is where soul winning begins.

Let the Church Weep Again

God doesn't need perfect words—He needs broken hearts. When we cry out for the lost, we are closest to His heart.

Bold Witnessing in a Fearful Culture

> "And when they had prayed... they were all filled with the Holy Ghost, and they spake the word of God with boldness." —Acts 4:31 (KJV)

We are living in a time where boldness is rare, and silence is popular. Fear has muzzled many believers. Culture has pressured the church to stay quiet. But the gospel is not a private message—it's a public declaration.

God is raising up a church that will be bold again. Not reckless, not arrogant—but unapologetically Spirit-led and gospel-focused.

Fear Is Not of God

> "For God hath not given us the spirit of fear..." —2 Timothy 1:7 (KJV)

Fear causes us to:

- Delay obedience.
- Avoid confrontation.
- Apologize for truth.

Reigniting the Fire of Soul Winning in Our Churches

- Stay silent when we should speak.

But the early church was not afraid of backlash, prison, or even death. They knew their witness was a heavenly assignment, not an earthly opinion.

Boldness Comes from the Holy Spirit

You don't manufacture boldness—you receive it.

> **"Ye shall receive power, after that the Holy Ghost is come upon you: and ye shall be witnesses…" —Acts 1:8 (KJV)**

Before Pentecost, Peter denied Christ. After Pentecost, he preached to thousands. The only difference? The fire of the Spirit.

The Church Must Speak Again

- Speak truth in love (see Ephesians 4:15).
- Speak clearly and boldly (see Acts 28:31).
- Speak when it's uncomfortable (see 2 Timothy 4:2).
- Speak even when you are rejected (see John 15:18–20).

The gospel doesn't need to be edited—it needs to be proclaimed.

A Call to Bold Witnessing

The culture does not need a quiet church—it needs a clear one. A fearless one. A gospel-saturated one.

Let us not be ashamed. Let us not retreat. Let us stand in streets, sanctuaries, and social circles declaring:

> **"I am not ashamed of the gospel of Christ: for it is the power of God unto salvation…" —Romans 1:16 (KJV)**

Church, be bold again. The world is waiting.

Becoming a Church on Fire

> **"But his word was in mine heart as a burning fire shut up in my bones…" —Jeremiah 20:9 (KJV)**

There's a vast difference between a church that is full and a church that is on fire. Full churches are common, but burning churches change cities. A church on fire cannot be ignored, silenced, or satisfied with routine. It is a church consumed by the presence of God and compelled by the urgency of the gospel.

This is the kind of church Jesus is returning for—not lukewarm, not trendy, but blazing with holy fire.

What Does a Church on Fire Look Like?

- It's consumed with God's presence – Worship is not a performance but an encounter.
- It's burdened for souls – Evangelism isn't optional; it's instinctive.
- It's bold in truth – The Word is preached without compromise.
- It's marked by prayer – Intercession fuels the atmosphere.
- It's passionate, not passive – People don't attend—they participate.

> **"Who maketh his angels spirits, and his ministers a flame of fire." —Hebrews 1:7 (KJV)**

God doesn't just want burning individuals—He wants burning churches.

You Can Feel the Fire

You can walk into a room and sense the difference:

- When fire is present, people are convicted.
- When fire is present, chains break.
- When fire is present, souls are saved.
- When fire is present, revival erupts.

This isn't emotionalism. It's supernatural intensity fueled by divine purpose.

Carriers of the Fire: When God Shows Up Through People

> **"But his word was in mine heart as a burning fire shut up in my bones…" —Jeremiah 20:9 (KJV)**

You don't have to announce fire. You feel it. You witness its fruit. You see it shift the room. These aren't performers—they're conduits. These are the people God uses to bring the fire that convicts, frees, saves, and revives.

1. **The Conviction Carrier – The One Who Shakes the Room with Truth**

> "Now when they heard this, they were pricked in their heart…" —Acts 2:37 (KJV)

This person doesn't even have to raise their voice. When they speak, conviction fills the air. They carry a prophetic weight that bypasses emotions and strikes the conscience. They don't seek attention—they carry authority.

Traits

- Piercing in truth.
- Discerning in spirit.
- Anchored in the Word.
- Graced to call people to repentance with clarity and love.

Altar calls follow them naturally. Their messages pierce hearts and bring repentance.

Challenge

Are you so filled with God's Word that people feel Him when you speak?

2. The Chain Breaker – The One Who Carries Deliverance Power

> "For unclean spirits, crying with loud voice, came out of many… and there was great joy in that city." —Acts 8:7–8 (KJV)

Reigniting the Fire of Soul Winning in Our Churches

This fire carrier walks into rooms where people have been bound for years, and suddenly, the chains fall. They don't perform deliverance—they walk in an atmosphere of authority.

Traits

- Spiritually sharp.
- Fearless in warfare.
- Gentle with the oppressed.
- Bold to confront the demonic.

Impact

Demonic activity is exposed. Mental strongholds crumble. People walk away free and whole.

Challenge

Are you spiritually sensitive enough to recognize bondage, and bold enough to confront it?

3. **The Soul-Winner – The One Who Draws People to Christ Without Striving**

   "**Come, see a man…**" —**John 4:29 (KJV)**

When this person talks, people listen. They don't manipulate—they magnetize. Their love is genuine. Their fire is focused on eternity. Souls are saved in restaurants, airports, and grocery stores because the gospel flows from them constantly.

Pastor Dr. Claudine Benjamin

Traits

- Consumed with compassion.
- Clear in the message of salvation.
- Bold but relational.
- Ready in every moment.

Impact

People often say, "I don't know what it is about you... but I feel something." That something is someone—the Holy Spirit.

Challenge

Is your life preaching Christ louder than your voice?

4. **The Revival Spark – The One Who Ignites the Atmosphere**

   "It came even to pass, as the trumpeters and singers were as one... the priests could not stand to minister by reason of the cloud: for the glory of the Lord had filled the house of God." —2 Chronicles 5:13–14 (KJV)

Some people don't just walk in fire—they ignite it in others. When this person steps up, atmospheres shift. Worship deepens. Tears fall. Laughter and healing break out. They are revival spark plugs—used by God to awaken sleeping churches.

Traits

- Sensitive to spiritual timing.
- Operates in prophetic worship or exhortation.

- Quick to obey the Spirit.
- Willing to be misunderstood for the sake of obedience.

Impact

The atmosphere is awakened. What was cold becomes hungry. What was rigid becomes fluid. Revival begins with one obedient flame.

Challenge

Will you burn bright even if others are content to stay lukewarm?

5. The Silent Burner – The One Whose Life Is on Fire, Even in Quiet

"The fire shall ever be burning upon the altar; it shall never go out." —Leviticus 6:13 (KJV)

Not every fire carrier shouts or leads. Some simply burn with holy consistency. Their devotion is deep. Their walk is pure. They don't chase platforms—they chase God. And in their prayer closet, the fire grows.

Traits

- Steady in the Word.
- Hidden but faithful.
- Intimate with God.
- Full of quiet power.

Pastor Dr. Claudine Benjamin

Impact

They shape atmospheres without speaking. Their prayers fuel altars. Their lives call others higher. They don't just talk revival—they live it.

Challenge

Will you carry fire even if no one claps for it?

The Fire Is Felt—Not Faked

You can't fake conviction.
You can't rehearse deliverance.
You can't manufacture salvations.
You can't script revival.
You must carry it.

> **"Did not our heart burn within us… while he opened to us the scriptures?" —Luke 24:32 (KJV)**

The fire of God is real. It's weighty. It's holy. And when someone truly carries it—you feel it.

God Is Not Visiting the Church for Entertainment—He's Looking for Fire

> **"Remember therefore from whence thou art fallen, and repent… or else I will come… and remove thy candlestick…" —Revelation 2:5 (KJV)**

If the fire dies, the light goes out. God is calling the church to burn again—for holiness, for souls, for His glory.

Sending the Church Out Again

"...as my Father hath sent me, even so send I you." — John 20:21 (KJV)

We were never meant to gather only—we were meant to go. The church is not a holding tank for saints. It's a launchpad for laborers. Somewhere along the way, the church became a destination instead of a deployment center. But the fire of revival doesn't stay behind stained glass—it flows into streets, homes, schools, and workplaces.

God is calling the church to move again.

CHAPTER 21

WE ARE A SENT PEOPLE

Jesus didn't just come to save us—He came to send us.

"Go ye into all the world, and preach the gospel to every creature." —Mark 16:15 (KJV)

Every believer is a missionary. Every workplace is a field. Every neighborhood is a harvest zone.

We've trained people to come to church. Now we must train them to go as the church.

Mobilizing the Church

To send the church out again:

- Preach the urgency of the harvest.
- Equip believers to witness where they are.
- Celebrate outreach stories and testimonies.
- Shift ministry focus outward—not just inward.

"The harvest truly is plenteous, but the labourers are few." —Matthew 9:37 (KJV)

If the laborers are few, it's because the church has focused more on feeding than sending.

From Maintenance to Mission

Churches on fire are not preoccupied with:

- Internal politics.
- Shallow preferences.
- Entertainment-driven services.

They are consumed with kingdom assignment.

Let the church leave the building. Let us go again. Let us send again.

Revival Through Evangelism

> **"And the Lord added to the church daily such as should be saved." —Acts 2:47 (KJV)**

Revival is not only about what happens inside the church—it's about who comes into the kingdom. We cannot call it revival if souls are not being saved. Every historic revival in scripture and history has been marked by the same thing: a harvest of souls.

Evangelism is not just the fruit of revival—it is often the fuel.

True Revival Bears Fruit

We must measure revival not by:

- Emotional highs.
- Extended services.
- New songs.

…but by repentance, conversions, and transformed lives.

> **"Then Philip went down to the city of Samaria, and preached Christ unto them. And there was great joy in that city." —Acts 8:5, 8 (KJV)**

Cities rejoice when Christ is preached. Revival brings joy—not just in the church, but in the community.

Evangelism Unlocks the Floodgates

When the church steps into soul winning:

- The Spirit begins to move more freely.
- God confirms the Word with signs (see Mark 16:20).
- The kingdom expands.
- Revival gains momentum.

Evangelism forces the church out of apathy and into spiritual war, and it's there that God shows up with power.

Revival Is Here—If We'll Reach for It

God is not waiting for better lighting or music. He's waiting for obedience. When we go out, God shows up.

Let revival be measured by souls. Let the fire fall in our preaching and our living. Let the gospel be preached again with urgency and power.

Church, revival is not coming—it's waiting. And evangelism is the doorway.

CHAPTER 22

THE CHURCH HAS LOST THE FIRE FOR SOUL WINNING

There was a time when the altars were filled, when street corners became pulpits, and when believers wept over lost souls. The church once carried a holy urgency—a relentless passion for soul winning. Evangelism wasn't a ministry department; it was the mission of the church. The cry for the lost echoed in prayer meetings, in Sunday sermons, and in the hearts of ordinary believers. But now, in many places, the fire has gone out.

Today, many churches have traded the great commission for great productions. Soul winning has become a side note instead of the headline. The fire that once burned hot has grown dim under the weight of apathy, distraction, and a culture more concerned with comfort than conversion.

Symptoms of a Church That's Lost Its Fire

1. Empty Altars and Silent Invitations

When was the last time people flooded the altar, broken before the Lord in repentance? When was the last time a church service ended with a soul genuinely coming to Christ? In many places, altar calls are either absent or rushed—reduced to polite invitations instead of passionate appeals.

Reigniting the Fire of Soul Winning in Our Churches

2. More Events, Less Evangelism

Many churches have become event-driven rather than mission-driven. Conferences, concerts, and programs abound—but how many of them are producing salvations? If souls aren't being saved, we must ask: What are we building?

3. Complacency Among Believers

The early church could not remain silent. The fire of the Holy Ghost compelled them to witness, even in persecution. Today, many believers go years without leading a single soul to Christ. Evangelism has become optional, inconvenient, or simply forgotten.

4. Doctrinal Drift and Diluted Messages

A gospel that no longer convicts cannot convert. In trying to be "relevant," many pulpits have grown silent on sin, repentance, and eternity. When truth is watered down to avoid offense, the fire goes with it. A church that no longer preaches about hell will not burn with passion to rescue people from it.

How Did We Lose the Fire?

1. By Replacing the Holy Spirit with Human Strategies

The early church was birthed in fire—the fire of the Holy Spirit. Today, many churches rely more on marketing teams than intercessory teams. We strategize before we seek. We plan before we pray. But no strategy can substitute for the anointing. The fire falls where hunger lives.

2. By Making Church About Us

When church becomes a place to be entertained instead of a place to be empowered, the fire fades. We sing about blessings but say little about brokenness. We seek feel-good sermons rather than soul-stirring truth. We want full pews, but forget that heaven rejoices over one sinner who repents (see Luke 15:7).

3. By Ignoring the Reality of Eternity

Heaven is real. Hell is real. Eternity is final. But the modern church seldom speaks of these truths. When we lose sight of eternal consequences, we lose urgency. If we truly believed people were one breath away from an eternity without Christ, we would not remain silent.

God's Heart Still Burns for Souls

While many in the church have grown cold, God's heart still burns with fire for the lost. He is still the seeking Shepherd. He is still the Father who runs to meet the prodigal. He is still the Redeemer who went to the cross for every soul.

The fire may have faded in our churches, but it has not faded in heaven. Jesus is still calling. The Holy Spirit is still convicting. The Father is still waiting. The harvest is still ripe.

The Fire Must Be Rekindled

1. Through Repentance

We must repent for neglecting the mission. We must fall on our faces and ask God to forgive us for being distracted, comfortable, and apathetic. Revival begins not with a program but with brokenness.

2. Through Prayer and Fasting

The fire returns through intimacy with God. As we seek Him, He purifies our hearts and reignites our passion. The early church prayed until the place shook. We must pray until our hearts burn again.

3. Through Preaching the Full Gospel

We must preach Jesus—the crucified, risen, returning King. We must preach repentance, holiness, salvation, and eternity. When the message is right, the fire will fall.

4. Through Evangelistic Action

Nothing fans the flame like leading a soul to Jesus. Evangelism keeps the fire alive. When the church begins to win souls again, we will see miracles, revival, and transformation. The gospel was never meant to be kept—it was meant to be carried.

A Church on Fire Cannot Be Ignored

When the church regains its fire for soul winning:

- The lost will come running.
- The bound will be set free.
- The lukewarm will awaken.

- The supernatural will follow.

When the Church Burns: The People Who Rise from the Flame

"Is not my word like as a fire? saith the Lord." — Jeremiah 23:29 (KJV)

When the church regains its fire, she doesn't simply get louder—she gets unstoppable. She becomes a sending center, a healing station, a rescue outpost. When a church burns with the fire of soul winning, God raises up a supernatural people.

1. The Evangelist Who Attracts the Lost – The Flame That Draws

"And I, if I be lifted up from the earth, will draw all men unto me." —John 12:32 (KJV)

This person doesn't just go looking for the lost—the lost come looking for them. Their life is lit with light, their words are seasoned with salt, and their spirit carries compassion and urgency. When they speak, sinners listen. When they walk into a room, conviction follows.

Traits

- Lives and breathes the gospel.
- Finds divine appointments everywhere.
- Radiates love and mercy.
- Carries a strong sense of eternity.

Reigniting the Fire of Soul Winning in Our Churches

People give their lives to Christ not because they're pressured, but because they're pursued with power.

Challenge

When people see you, do they feel drawn to Jesus?

2. The Deliverer – The Flame That Breaks Chains

> "…he hath sent me to heal the brokenhearted, to preach deliverance to the captives…" —Luke 4:18 (KJV)

This fiery vessel walks in the authority of the name of Jesus and confronts spiritual bondage without fear. Whether it's addiction, demonic oppression, or emotional strongholds—when they pray, the chains fall.

Traits

- Deep in prayer, bold in battle.
- Walks in discernment.
- Compassionate toward the broken.
- Skilled in Scripture and Spirit.

What counseling couldn't cure, this person's anointed prayer can break in a moment.

Challenge

Are you willing to carry the fire that sets others free, even when it costs you comfort?

3. The Awakener – The Flame That Revives the Lukewarm

> **"...strengthen the things which remain, that are ready to die..." —Revelation 3:2 (KJV)**

When the church is on fire, God raises up revival voices—those who call out compromise, confront apathy, and awaken the sleeping. These are the awakeners, stirred not by anger, but by burden. They won't allow the church to sleep while souls perish.

Traits

- Prophetically alert.
- Hates complacency, loves the church.
- Calls others to prayer, fasting, and consecration.
- Weeps over the lukewarm.

What was dead comes alive. What was dull becomes discerning. What was routine becomes revival.

Challenge

Are you willing to confront apathy to stir up the flame?

4. The Supernatural Believer – The Flame That Hosts Heaven

> **"And Stephen, full of faith and power, did great wonders and miracles among the people." —Acts 6:8 (KJV)**

This person isn't famous, but they're full of the Holy Spirit. They live naturally supernatural. Miracles happen not because they force them, but because heaven rests on them. The atmosphere shifts when they pray, worship, or walk into the room.

Reigniting the Fire of Soul Winning in Our Churches

Traits

- Spirit-led and Spirit-filled.
- Lives with constant expectation.
- Walks in humility and holiness.
- Has faith for the impossible.

Miracles aren't rare. Healing flows. Dreams are birthed. The presence of God is normal around them.

Challenge

Do you carry an atmosphere of heaven, or just the appearance of religion?

5. **The Church That Cannot Be Ignored – The Flame That Engulfs a City**

   "And fear came upon every soul: and many wonders and signs were done by the apostles." —Acts 2:43 (KJV)

When the church is ablaze:

- The lost come running.
- The bound are set free.
- The lukewarm awaken.
- The supernatural follows.

This isn't a building—it's a burning altar, a spiritual embassy, a divine invasion site. This kind of church shakes cities, reclaims streets, and births movements.

Traits

- Intercession fuels the foundation.
- Discipleship is serious.
- Evangelism is daily.
- The Holy Spirit is fully welcomed.

No one in the city can ignore it. Not because it's flashy, but because it's full of fire.

Challenge

Is your church a place of revival or just a place of routine?

Burn Bright and Be Bold

A church on fire doesn't beg for relevance. It doesn't chase trends. It doesn't compromise. Instead, it becomes:

- A beacon to the lost.
- A bomb shelter for the broken.
- A battalion for kingdom laborers.
- A blaze that sparks national revival.

CHAPTER 23

A CHURCH ON FIRE CANNOT BE IGNORED

"Is not my word like as a fire? saith the Lord." —Jeremiah 23:29 (KJV)

Fire doesn't whisper—it roars. It consumes. It draws attention. And when the church catches fire—not with performance, but with power—the world cannot help but look. It doesn't matter how small the building or how humble the people, when the church burns with the fire of the Holy Spirit, it becomes undeniable and unstoppable.

Today, God is calling His church out of religious routine and back into revival. He's looking for a people who burn with compassion for the lost and burn with courage to preach the gospel in power.

When the fire returns to the church, four undeniable things begin to happen:

1. **The Lost Will Come Running**

   "And the Lord added to the church daily such as should be saved." —Acts 2:47 (KJV)

Reigniting the Fire of Soul Winning in Our Churches

A church on fire attracts those drowning in darkness. You don't have to beg the lost to come when the Spirit is moving with conviction and clarity—they will come looking for the light.

Why? Because when fire is present:

- The gospel is preached with power.
- Sin is confronted with grace.
- Love is not shallow—it's transforming.
- People don't feel judged—they feel drawn.

Jesus said:

> **"And I, if I be lifted up from the earth, will draw all men unto me." —John 12:32 (KJV)**

When Christ is exalted, and the Spirit is free to move, the lost will respond.

2. The Bound Will Be Set Free

> **"…to proclaim liberty to the captives, and the opening of the prison to them that are bound." —Isaiah 61:1 (KJV)**

Where the fire of God is present, bondage cannot survive. Chains of addiction, fear, depression, and demonic oppression are broken—not through emotional hype, but by anointed authority.

In a fire-filled church:

- Deliverance happens at the altar.

- Strongholds are broken in worship.
- Demons flee at the name of Jesus.
- Lives are changed without fanfare—just fire.

Jesus came to set captives free, and He still does—through a church that hosts His fire.

3. The Lukewarm Will Awaken

> **"I know thy works, that thou art neither cold nor hot... I will spue thee out of my mouth." —Revelation 3:15–16 (KJV)**

Lukewarm Christianity thrives where there is no fire. But when the Spirit of God truly moves, lukewarm hearts are exposed—and invited to burn again.

In a church on fire:

- Complacency becomes conviction.
- Passive believers become passionate laborers.
- Shallow religion is replaced with deep surrender.
- The sleeping bride wakes up and takes her place.

The early church was ablaze with holy urgency. Every prayer meeting was filled. Every member was a witness. And every gathering carried a weight of glory.

> **"...it is high time to awake out of sleep..." —Romans 13:11 (KJV)**

4. The Supernatural Will Follow

> "And these signs shall follow them that believe…" — **Mark 16:17 (KJV)**

The fire is never for entertainment. It's for equipping and empowering. When the church is truly on fire, the supernatural isn't rare—it's expected.

— Healings occur in services and streets.
— Prophetic words bring clarity and breakthrough.
— Tongues, visions, and miracles become normal.
— Worship is no longer performance—it's encounter.

The supernatural isn't weird in a burning church—it's welcomed.

The early church walked in power because they walked in intimacy with the Holy Spirit. Fire precedes fruit. Prayer precedes power. Surrender precedes signs.

> "And with great power gave the apostles witness of the resurrection of the Lord Jesus: and great grace was upon them all." —**Acts 4:33 (KJV)**

Let the Fire Fall Again

The church does not need more:

- Programs
- Pulpit personalities
- Polished services

What it desperately needs is:

- Power that pierces darkness.
- Purity that produces credibility.
- Passion that fuels soul winning.
- Presence that awakens the altar.

A church on fire cannot be ignored because heaven walks in when the people burn.

Let your church become:

- The place where sinners run to the altar.
- The place where the addicted are set free.
- The place where the sleeping are revived.
- The place where miracles aren't planned—but happen.

> **"And the fire shall ever be burning upon the altar; it shall never go out." —Leviticus 6:13 (KJV)**

The church that burns will be the church that harvests.

> **"Let your light so shine before men…" —Matthew 5:16 (KJV)**

The fire is not for fame. It's for souls.

A fire-filled church is a threat to hell and a hope to the world. It doesn't blend in—it stands out. It doesn't play it safe—it steps out in faith.

A Call to the Church Today

"Nevertheless I have somewhat against thee, because thou hast left thy first love. Remember therefore from whence thou art fallen, and repent..." —Revelation 2:4–5 (KJV)

Church, it's time to return.

— We've built beautiful sanctuaries—but lost the sanctuary of prayer.
— We've built platforms—but lost the posture of brokenness.
— We've gained popularity—but forfeited power.
— We've gained crowds—but lost the commission.

This is not a call to nostalgia—it's a call to obedience. A call to realign with heaven's heart. A call to drop our tools, tear our programs, and return to what burns.

1. Return to the Mission

"Go ye into all the world, and preach the gospel to every creature." —Mark 16:15 (KJV)

The mission has never changed—but we have. The great commission has become the great omission in many churches. We've shifted from soul winning to service planning, from sending to settling, from reaching the lost to entertaining the found.

But Jesus never commissioned us to build comfortable communities—He commissioned us to rescue the dying.

A church that has forgotten the mission:

- Measures success by attendance, not transformation.
- Builds up ministries but forgets the harvest.
- Fills calendars but ignores the great commission.

A church that returns to the mission:

- Makes soul winning a culture, not a department.
- Equips every believer as a laborer.
- Measures growth by disciples, not followers.

> **"For the Son of man is come to seek and to save that which was lost." —Luke 19:10 (KJV)**

The mission is not optional. It's the heartbeat of Jesus.

2. Return to the Altar

> **"And Elijah… repaired the altar of the Lord that was broken down." —1 Kings 18:30 (KJV)**

Before revival came on Mount Carmel, Elijah had to repair the altar. Today, many churches have altars in name only—decorative spaces rather than places of deep surrender.

The altar is not just a spot at the front of the church. It's where:

- Sin is confessed.
- Deliverance begins.
- Fire falls.

- God speaks.

A church that returns to the altar:

- Makes room for people to linger in God's presence.
- Refuses to rush repentance.
- Train leaders who lead from brokenness, not pride.

> **"The fire shall ever be burning upon the altar; it shall never go out." —Leviticus 6:13 (KJV)**

If we want the fire, we must rebuild the altar.

3. **Return to the Fire**

> **"...he shall baptize you with the Holy Ghost, and with fire." —Matthew 3:11 (KJV)**

The church was born in fire. Tongues of fire rested on each one (see Acts 2:3), and from that moment forward, they burned with holy urgency. They didn't need lights, branding, or popularity. They had fire, and it was enough.

But in many churches today:

- Fire has been replaced with form.
- Passion has been replaced with performance.
- Power has been replaced with professionalism.

We need the fire again:

- Fire that purifies.
- Fire that empowers.
- Fire that sends.

"Wherefore I put thee in remembrance that thou stir up the gift of God…" —2 Timothy 1:6 (KJV)

You don't find the fire by watching others—you stir it by seeking God until it comes.

4. The World Doesn't Need More Impressive Buildings—It Needs Burning Hearts

"Did not our heart burn within us…?" —Luke 24:32 (KJV)

We've built cathedrals but lost the upper room. We've perfected acoustics but lost the echo of intercession. God is not impressed by architecture—He is drawn to altars set aflame by yielded lives.

The world is not waiting for another modern church—it's longing for a burning one.

What burning hearts do:

- Chase souls, not trends.
- Live surrendered, not polished.
- Speak with authority, not popularity.

Reigniting the Fire of Soul Winning in Our Churches

- Love with fire, not flattery.

When the church regains its burn, the lost will come running.

5. It Needs Fearless Witnesses

> "And they overcame him by the blood of the Lamb, and by the word of their testimony…" —Revelation 12:11 (KJV)

Fear has silenced many pulpits. Timidity has paralyzed many pews. But the early church witnessed through persecution, prison, and death. Why? Because they had seen too much to stay silent.

We need:

- Teenagers preaching in schools.
- Businessmen evangelizing in boardrooms.
- Mothers praying down revival in neighborhoods.
- Pastors declaring truth in love, even when it offends.

We don't need louder personalities—we need unshakable witnesses.

> "For we cannot but speak the things which we have seen and heard." —Acts 4:20 (KJV)

6. It Needs a Church on Fire for the Souls Jesus Died to Save

> "He shall see of the travail of his soul, and shall be satisfied…" —Isaiah 53:11 (KJV)

Jesus didn't die to build empires. He died to save souls. He is worthy of the reward of His suffering. And that reward is not full churches—it's saved people.

The church on fire doesn't forget:

- That hell is real.
- That eternity is close.
- That the gospel still works.
- That salvation is urgent.

> **"And of some have compassion, making a difference: And others save with fear, pulling them out of the fire…"**
> **—Jude 1:22–23 (KJV)**

Church, Come Back to the Flame

This is a call—not to religion, but to fire.
Not to performance, but to power.
Not to growth without glory—but to souls that shake eternity.

Let us return:

- To the mission that reaches.
- To the altar that burns.
- To the fire that sends.
- To the boldness that testifies.
- To the burden that weeps for the lost.

Church, it's time. Not tomorrow—now.

Reigniting the Fire of Soul Winning in Our Churches

The world is groaning. Heaven is waiting. Hell is raging.

Let the church burn again.

> **"Wilt thou not revive us again: that thy people may rejoice in thee?" —Psalm 85:6 (KJV)**

Declaration

We are the church. We will not be silent. We will not be cold. We will burn again with holy fire. We will preach the gospel. We will call the lost home. We will not rest until our altars are full, our streets are reached, and our communities are changed. The fire is returning—and we say yes.

CHAPTER 24

THE CHURCH ON FIRE FOR THE HARVEST

The church was never meant to be a monument—it was meant to be a movement. Not a place where flames fade, but where fire spreads. A church on fire is a church alive, awakened, and ablaze with heaven's purpose. It's a church consumed with one holy obsession: to see the lost saved, the broken restored, and the gospel preached to every soul, in every place, at every cost.

In Acts 2, the early church was born in fire. The Holy Spirit descended like flames, and what followed was not a quiet service, but an outbreak of power, preaching, and people repenting. That fire didn't remain in the upper room—it spilled into the streets, the synagogues, the cities, and eventually the nations. That's what happens when the church catches fire. The harvest becomes the priority, and the world becomes the mission field.

Today, that same fire is available. That same Holy Spirit still ignites. But the question remains: Will the church burn again?

What Does It Mean for the Church to Be "on Fire"?

A church on fire is not measured by lights, sound, or crowds. It is measured by eternal impact. It's a church that:

Reigniting the Fire of Soul Winning in Our Churches

- Is consumed with the mission of Christ.
- Refuses to grow cold or complacent.
- Is sensitive to the Holy Spirit's leading.
- Is marked by fervent prayer, bold preaching, and relentless evangelism.
- Has altars that are never empty and streets that are never ignored.

The fire of God doesn't settle in places of passivity—it ignites where there is hunger, humility, and holiness.

A church that is truly ablaze with the fire of God has returned to its first love, reignited its passion for the lost, and is driven by an unquenchable burden to see souls saved. This kind of church is not content with religious routine but is hungry for revival, ready for reformation, and desperate for divine intervention.

Consumed With the Mission of Christ

Such a church lives and breathes the great commission. It doesn't treat soul winning as optional but sees it as its highest calling. The passion of Christ becomes its pursuit.

> **"Go ye therefore, and teach all nations, baptizing them in the name of the Father, and of the Son, and of the Holy Ghost." —Matthew 28:19 (KJV)**

> **"For the Son of man is come to seek and to save that which was lost." —Luke 19:10 (KJV)**

Refuses to Grow Cold or Complacent

The fire of revival cannot coexist with lukewarmness. A soul-winning church stays on fire by fanning the flames of urgency and weeping for the lost. It resists the trap of comfort and continually stirs itself to action.

> "Nevertheless I have somewhat against thee, because thou hast left thy first love. Remember therefore from whence thou art fallen, and repent..." —Revelation 2:4–5 (KJV)

> "Woe to them that are at ease in Zion..." —Amos 6:1 (KJV)

Sensitive to the Holy Spirit's Leading

It is not driven by programs, but by the power and prompting of the Holy Ghost. This church moves when He says move, speaks when He says speak, and surrenders completely to His guidance.

> "But ye shall receive power, after that the Holy Ghost is come upon you: and ye shall be witnesses unto me..." —Acts 1:8 (KJV)

> "As many as are led by the Spirit of God, they are the sons of God." —Romans 8:14 (KJV)

Marked by Fervent Prayer, Bold Preaching, and Relentless Evangelism

Revival fire is sustained in the furnace of prayer. It is fueled by bold, uncompromising preaching and expressed through continuous outreach. A soul-winning church spends more time interceding for the lost than entertaining the found.

> "The effectual fervent prayer of a righteous man availeth much." —James 5:16b (KJV)

> "Preach the word; be instant in season, out of season; reprove, rebuke, exhort…" —2 Timothy 4:2 (KJV)

> "And daily in the temple, and in every house, they ceased not to teach and preach Jesus Christ." —Acts 5:42 (KJV)

Has Altars That Are Never Empty and Streets That Are Never Ignored

In a soul-winning church, the altar is a place of tears, repentance, deliverance, and new beginnings. However, the burden doesn't stay confined to four walls—it spills over into neighborhoods, cities, and nations.

> "Blow the trumpet in Zion, sanctify a fast, call a solemn assembly. Let the priests, the ministers of the Lord, weep between the porch and the altar…" —Joel 2:15, 17 (KJV)

> **"Go out quickly into the streets and lanes of the city, and bring in hither the poor, and the maimed, and the halt, and the blind." —Luke 14:21b (KJV)**

The Fire of God Doesn't Settle in Places of Passivity–It Ignites

God doesn't pour out His Spirit on stagnant places. He consumes what is yielded. The fire falls where there is hunger, obedience, and a willingness to be set ablaze. We must not merely talk about revival—we must become the fuel for it.

> **"Then the fire of the Lord fell, and consumed the burnt sacrifice…" —1 Kings 18:38a (KJV)**

> **"And of the angels he saith, Who maketh his angels spirits, and his ministers a flame of fire." —Hebrews 1:7 (KJV)**

> **"Wherefore I put thee in remembrance that thou stir up the gift of God, which is in thee by the putting on of my hands." —2 Timothy 1:6 (KJV)**

CHAPTER 25

REKINDLING THE FLAME OF EVANGELISM IN THE CHURCH

The true mark of a church that is on fire is not just what happens inside its walls—it's what it releases into the world. And nothing reflects the heart of a burning church more than evangelism. A church without evangelism is a church that has lost its purpose. A church that does not reach for the lost has forgotten the mission of its Savior.

Evangelism is not outdated. It's not optional. It's essential.

And yet, in many corners of today's church, the flame of evangelism has been reduced to a flicker. Outreach has been replaced with events. Soul winning has been outsourced to a few, while the rest watch from a distance. The altar call is rarely given, the streets are rarely touched, and the cry for the lost is rarely heard.

But the call has not changed. The commission has not expired. The fire still falls—but only on a church that is willing to go.

The Evangelism Fire Must Burn Again

Jesus came "to seek and to save that which was lost" (see Luke 19:10). That same urgency must burn in us. We are not here to merely steward blessings—we are here to rescue souls. The early church understood this. They risked everything to preach the gospel. Their message wasn't safe—it was Spirit-filled. Their mission wasn't comfortable—it was costly.

And yet, the modern church often plays it safe. We fear offense more than we fear the loss of a soul. We build ministries around attracting people, not sending them. But evangelism was never meant to be a department. It was meant to be a heartbeat.

Let us be reminded:

- Every saved person is a sent person.
- Every Christian is called to be a witness.
- Evangelism is not for the extroverted—it's for the obedient.

What Happened to the Fire?

- **We've replaced passion with professionalism.**

We've made church services smooth but have lost the rough edge of spiritual urgency. We know how to "do church," but we've forgotten how to be the church.

- **We've prioritized comfort over commission.**

Reaching the lost is inconvenient. It disrupts schedules, challenges our comfort zones, and requires sacrifice. But if we aren't willing to be uncomfortable, we aren't ready to be used.

- **We've become distracted.**

So many things compete for our attention—programs, platforms, politics, personalities. Meanwhile, souls are perishing while we're perfecting strategies.

Reviving Evangelism in the Church

To rekindle the flame of evangelism, the church must return to:

- **The Power of the Gospel**

We don't need to repackage the message—we need to release it. The gospel still saves. It still transforms. It still sets captives free.

- **The Urgency of Eternity**

Heaven is real. So is hell. And every person you pass today is going to one or the other. This should break our hearts and move our feet.

- **The Boldness of the Spirit**

Acts 4:31 tells us that after they prayed, the early church was filled with the Spirit and spoke the Word of God with boldness. We need this boldness again—not arrogance, but Holy Spirit courage to speak truth in love.

- **The Simplicity of Obedience**

Evangelism is often as simple as an invitation, a conversation, or a testimony. You don't need a microphone—you need a heart willing to be used.

Reigniting the Fire of Soul Winning in Our Churches

- **The Burden of Intercession**

Evangelism begins in prayer. We must pray for the lost by name. Cry out for the hardened hearts. Plead for revival. Before we can reach people, we must first weep for them.

Let the Flame Fall Again

We are not waiting on the world to be ready—the world is waiting on the church to burn again.

The fire of evangelism must rise:

- **In the pulpits**—with bold altar calls and gospel preaching.
- **In the pews**—with everyday believers who see every place as a mission field.
- **In the youth**—with a new generation unashamed of Christ.
- **In the streets**—with worship, witness, and works of love.
- **In every believer**—with a cry that says, "Lord, send me."

This Is Our Hour

God is stirring His church. The sound of revival is not just singing—it is souls coming to the Savior. The sign of a fiery church is not how high we shout, but how far we reach. And the evidence of the Spirit's fire is not just tongues of flame, but hearts that burn to see others saved.

Let us rise, church. Not later. Not next year. Now.

Pastor Dr. Claudine Benjamin

Let us be:

- Churches that preach the gospel without compromise.
- Believers who live the gospel without shame.
- Leaders who lead with passion and not performance.
- A people who will not let the fire go out again.

The harvest is ready. The time is now.

Let us go, let us burn, and let us win the lost at any cost.

"Here am I, Lord. Send me."

The Challenges the Church Faces Today

Comfort Culture

In many Western churches, convenience has replaced commitment. People attend if they "feel like it." Evangelism has become optional. The call to "go" has been softened by the desire to "gather."

But the gospel is not comfortable—it's confrontational. It demands that we die to ourselves so others might live. A church addicted to comfort will never be effective in the trenches of the harvest.

CHAPTER 26

WHEN THE FIRE FOR SOULS HAS GONE OUT

Perhaps the most sobering reason the labourers are few is not fear, comfort, or even distraction. It's indifference.

- Indifference says, "It's not my responsibility."
- Indifference says, "Someone else will reach them."
- Indifference sees the lost and walks the other way.

This is not just a challenge—it is a spiritual emergency.

When the Burden Is Gone, the Mission Stops

Romans 9:2–3 reveals Paul's heart: **"That I have great heaviness and continual sorrow in my heart. For I could wish that myself were accursed from Christ for my brethren, my kinsmen according to the flesh:" (KJV).**

Paul carried an intense burden for the lost. He didn't preach out of duty—he burned with divine urgency. But in much of today's church, this anguish has been replaced by apathy. We are no longer moved by the thought of souls perishing without Christ.

The question is no longer: *"Do we know the gospel?"* It's: *"Do we still care that others don't?"*

What Causes Spiritual Indifference?

- **Familiarity with the gospel.** The message becomes routine. We forget its power and its cost.

- **Focus on self over souls.** We center our faith around blessing, comfort, and personal growth—leaving no room for sacrifice.

- **Lack of intimacy with God.** When we lose connection to the heart of God, we stop feeling what He feels.

- **A cold and calloused culture.** Constant exposure to sin and tragedy without spiritual response numbs our sensitivity.

Signs of Indifference in the Church

- Evangelism is rarely mentioned.
- Altar calls are rushed or missing.
- Prayer for the lost is absent from gatherings.
- Leaders prioritize programs over people.
- Believers live without urgency for eternity.

Indifference doesn't look like rebellion—it looks like disengagement.

How to Restore the Fire for Souls

- **Return to the cross.** Let the reality of Christ's sacrifice for your soul reignite compassion for others.

- **Ask God to break your heart again.** Pray like this: "Lord, give me Your burden for the lost. Let me feel what You feel."

- **Expose yourself to need.** Evangelism begins when you see the pain, poverty, and brokenness of the harvest.

- **Preach and teach on eternity.** Hell is real. Heaven is real. Eternity is close. Indifference fades in the face of these truths.

- **Surround yourself with soul-winners.** Fire is contagious. Fellowship with those who burn for souls.

Return to the Cross

"But God commendeth his love toward us, in that, while we were yet sinners, Christ died for us." —Romans 5:8 (KJV)

The fire to reach others is not sustained by human effort—it is ignited and rekindled at the foot of the cross. When your passion fades, your compassion grows cold, or your heart becomes distracted, the solution is not to try harder. It's to look again at Jesus—bleeding, suffering, dying—not for a cause, but for your soul.

The cross is where love and urgency collide.

Let His Sacrifice Move You Again

"Greater love hath no man than this, that a man lay down his life for his friends." —John 15:13 (KJV)

When you remember how lost you were, how far He came to reach you, and how much it cost Him, something awakens. You can't truly see the cross and remain indifferent to others who still don't know that love.

Return to the cross by:

- Reading the crucifixion accounts in the gospels slowly and prayerfully.
- Spending time in personal worship focused solely on the Lamb who was slain.
- Thanking Jesus for specific things He delivered you from.
- Reflecting on what eternity would look like without the cross.

Reflection Questions

1. Have I lost sight of the cross in my everyday walk?

2. When was the last time the reality of Jesus' sacrifice moved me to tears or action?

Prayer

Jesus, I return to the cross. Let the price You paid for me ignite my passion to reach others. Don't let me forget what You rescued me from. Burn in me again. Amen.

Ask God to Break Your Heart Again

> **"A new heart also will I give you, and a new spirit will I put within you: and I will take away the stony heart out of your flesh, and I will give you an heart of flesh."** — **Ezekiel 36:26 (KJV)**

Sometimes the greatest danger in the Christian life is not sin, but numbness. A heart that once wept over souls now scrolls past suffering. A heart that once prayed for the lost now simply attends services.

If your fire has faded, it's time to ask: "Lord, break my heart again."

A Broken Heart is a Burdened Heart

God uses broken hearts to reach broken people. Revival doesn't start with shouting—it starts with weeping.

> **"Rivers of waters run down mine eyes, because they keep not thy law."** —**Psalm 119:136 (KJV)**

You will never cry out for souls until you feel what God feels.

Pray boldly and honestly:

- "Lord, show me what breaks Your heart."
- "Let me feel Your grief over the lost."
- "Don't let me grow cold to what matters most."

These are dangerous prayers because they will change your life.

Reigniting the Fire of Soul Winning in Our Churches

How God breaks our hearts:

- Through time in His presence.
- Through Scripture that convicts and awakens.
- Through exposure to need and suffering.
- Through reminders of your own deliverance.

Reflection Questions

1. Have I asked God to give me His burden for the lost?

2. Am I willing to be broken to be useful?

Prayer

Lord, give me Your heart. Break me out of comfort and coldness. Let me carry Your burden. Let me burn again with compassion. Don't let me grow numb. In Jesus' name. Amen.

Expose Yourself to Need

"But when he saw the multitudes, he was moved with compassion on them…" —Matthew 9:36 (KJV)

You will never feel the urgency of the harvest until you see it for yourself. If you want the fire for souls to return, you must step outside the sanctuary and into the streets, shelters, prisons, neighborhoods, and broken places where the harvest waits.

"Mine eye affecteth mine heart…" —Lamentations 3:51 (KJV)

What you see will shape what you feel.

Avoiding the Need Dulls the Fire

It's possible to be saved, anointed, and active in church, yet completely disconnected from the pain of the lost. Many churches have created bubbles of protection that unintentionally insulate their people from compassion.

You will never be burdened for what you refuse to look at.

Practical ways to see the harvest:

- Volunteer with outreach teams in your church.
- Visit places of brokenness—homeless shelters, jails, hospitals.
- Walk through your neighborhood and ask the Holy Spirit to open your eyes.
- Sit with unbelievers. Hear their stories without judgment.

Reflection Question

1. Have I protected myself from the pain of others so much that I no longer feel the need?

Prayer

Lord, open my eyes to the harvest. Help me to see past behavior into brokenness. Let me feel the weight of those who don't know You. Move me with compassion, like You were moved. Amen.

Preach and Teach on Eternity

> "And these shall go away into everlasting punishment: but the righteous into life eternal." —Matthew 25:46 (KJV)

Hell is real. Heaven is real. Eternity is not optional.

When the church stops talking about eternity, it stops evangelizing with urgency.

The fire for souls is rekindled when we remember what's at stake.

Hell Is Not a Metaphor

Jesus spoke more about hell than He did about heaven. Why? Because He came to save us from it. If hell is no longer part of our message, neither is the full gospel.

Every person you meet is either moving toward eternal life—or eternal separation from God. There is no middle ground.

Teach the Reality of Judgment

Remind your heart—and those you minister to—that:

1. **No second chances after death**

   > "And as it is appointed unto men once to die, but after this the judgment." —Hebrews 9:27 (KJV)

We live in a world that offers endless second chances—except for one. After death, there is no undoing, no renegotiation, no opportunity to repent. Eternity is sealed the moment life ends. Yet many in the church live as if there's always tomorrow.

The gospel we preach is not just good news—it's urgent news. Once a soul slips into eternity, their fate is final. That truth must drive us to speak, to share, and to compel.

2. Eternity is immediate

Jesus often warned about the finality of death:

- The rich man in Luke 16 begged for relief and for someone to warn his brothers, but it was too late.
- The foolish virgins in Matthew 25 found the door shut forever.
- The thief on the cross was saved because he cried out before death, not after.

"...the night cometh, when no man can work." —John 9:4 (KJV)

Time is limited. Opportunity ends. There is no evangelism in the graveyard.

The Church Must Live With Eternal Vision

If we truly understood that souls don't get second chances after death:

- Our priorities would shift.
- Our conversations would change.

Reigniting the Fire of Soul Winning in Our Churches

- Our worship would deepen.
- Our witness would intensify.

We would stop excusing silence and start acting with holy urgency.

> **"Knowing therefore the terror of the Lord, we persuade men…" —2 Corinthians 5:11 (KJV)**

Eternity must not be a side doctrine. It must be the lens through which we live.

The Harvest Is Urgent Because Time Is Short

> **"Say not ye, There are yet four months, and then cometh harvest? behold, I say unto you, Lift up your eyes, and look on the fields; for they are white already to harvest." —John 4:35 (KJV)**

We often think there's more time. More days. More chances. But Jesus said, "Don't wait." The harvest isn't coming—it's already here.

The lie of "later" has kept the church passive while people perish. The urgency of the harvest must be rediscovered.

Why Is the Harvest Urgent?

- **People are dying daily** – Thousands enter eternity every hour.
- **Hearts harden over time** – Delay gives sin and deception more ground.
- **Jesus is coming soon** – The time of mercy is limited.

- **Opportunities don't last forever** – The person you're avoiding today might not be reachable tomorrow.

> **"Redeeming the time, because the days are evil." — Ephesians 5:16 (KJV)**

Time is not guaranteed. The harvest spoils if we don't act.

Excuses Kill Evangelism

Excuses sound like:

- "I'll invite them next week."
- "I'm not ready yet."
- "They already know where I stand."
- "Someone else will reach them."

But heaven counts missed moments. We must be willing to interrupt our routine for divine assignments.

> **"Boast not thyself of to morrow; for thou knowest not what a day may bring forth." —Proverbs 27:1 (KJV)**

Today Is the Day

> **"…behold, now is the accepted time; behold, now is the day of salvation." —2 Corinthians 6:2 (KJV)**

We are not promised another season. The harvest is perishable. And we are the laborers sent to bring it in—now.

Evangelism Is Not Optional—It's Rescue Work

> **"And others save with fear, pulling them out of the fire…"** —Jude 1:23 (KJV)

Evangelism isn't a suggestion. It's a spiritual emergency response. We are not offering advice—we are offering a lifeline. When the church sees evangelism as optional, the lost remain unreached, and the mission is neglected.

This isn't about personal passion—it's about kingdom responsibility.

Evangelism Is Spiritual Rescue

Picture a burning building. Imagine people trapped inside. Would you:

- Debate the fire?
- Wait for better training?
- Worry about being offensive?

No. You would go in. You would call out. You would rescue.

That is evangelism.

> **"Who will have all men to be saved, and to come unto the knowledge of the truth."** —1 Timothy 2:4 (KJV)

This is what God desires—and we are His messengers.

Pastor Dr. Claudine Benjamin

Why It Cannot Be Optional

- Because Jesus commanded it (see Matthew 28:19).
- Because hell is real (see Luke 16:23).
- Because someone once reached you.
- Because you were saved to serve (see Ephesians 2:10).

To ignore the lost is to reject the very heart of God.

> **"For the Son of man is come to seek and to save that which was lost." —Luke 19:10 (KJV)**

If that was Jesus' mission, it must be ours.

The Church Must Shift from Volunteerism to Vocation

This is not for the "evangelism team" only. Every believer is called. Every voice matters. Every testimony is a weapon.

You don't need a title to testify. You don't need a pulpit to preach. You just need to obey.

Let the church rise again—not as spectators, but as rescuers. Evangelism is not a side project—it is a rescue mission with eternal consequences.

Souls don't get a second chance. Time is running out. We must go now.

> **"Go out into the highways and hedges, and compel them to come in…" —Luke 14:23 (KJV)**

CHAPTER 27

HOLINESS

Fire does not fall on the proud. It does not rest on the passive. It does not ignite where there is complacency. The fire of God falls where there is hunger, humility, and holiness. These are the conditions that invite revival. These are the ingredients of a church that burns.

Hunger: The Cry for More

Matthew 5:6 says: **"Blessed are they which do hunger and thirst after righteousness: for they shall be filled." (KJV).**

Spiritual hunger is not a wish—it is a desperate desire. It is a soul that says, *"God, I cannot go another moment without You."* A church on fire is made up of people who are not content with yesterday's touch or last year's breakthrough. They long for more of God—more of His presence, more of His glory, more of His Word, more of His power.

Hunger moves us beyond comfort. It presses us into prayer. It births revival.

Humility: The Posture of Revival

2 Chronicles 7:14 says: **"If my people, which are called by my name, shall humble themselves, and pray, and seek my face, and**

turn from their wicked ways; then will I hear from heaven, and will forgive their sin, and will heal their land." (KJV).

God does not move where pride reigns. The fire falls on the humble—those who recognize their need for God, those who do not seek glory for themselves but point all glory to Him.

Humility is not weakness—it is surrender. It's admitting, *"I am nothing without You."* It's laying down our titles, our status, and our control. A church on fire is a church on its knees.

Holiness: The Atmosphere Where God Dwells

Hebrews 12:14 reminds us: **"Follow peace with all men, and holiness, without which no man shall see the Lord:" (KJV).**

Holiness is not legalism—it is alignment with the heart of God. It is purity in action, motive, and thought. It is saying "yes" to righteousness and "no" to sin.

The fire of God is holy. It consumes sin. It purifies hearts. It burns away what is unclean. If we want the fire, we must be willing to let it refine us.

A fiery church doesn't just sing about the presence of God—it creates a place where He is welcome. Holiness makes room for the fire.

Revival Is Conditional

We often pray for fire, but fire has conditions. In the Old Testament, Elijah repaired the altar, laid the sacrifice in order, and soaked it with water before fire fell from heaven (see 1 Kings 18). Preparation precedes fire.

The fire of God will fall on the church that is:

- Hungry enough to seek Him.
- Humble enough to admit it needs Him.
- Holy enough to host Him.

Living Altars Attract Living Fire

Romans 12:1 calls us to present our bodies as living sacrifices—this is where the fire falls. It's not about perfect people, but yielded people. It's not about tradition—it's about transformation.

If we want sustained fire, we must build a sustained altar of hunger, humility, and holiness.

Lord, Send the Fire Again

This is where it all comes together. A church that is consumed with Christ's mission, refuses complacency, follows the Spirit, prays fervently, preaches boldly, evangelizes relentlessly, serves the streets, keeps the altar full, and walks in hunger, humility, and holiness—that church will never burn out.

That church will burn brightly.

Let us be the generation that doesn't just talk about revival but lives in it. Let us prepare the altar, bring the sacrifice, and cry out: *"Lord, send the fire again!"*

It Numbs the Burden

> **"Mine eye affecteth mine heart…" —Lamentations 3:51 (KJV)**

Before evangelism becomes action, it begins as a burden. A holy weight. A spiritual ache. A fire in your bones that makes it impossible to stay silent when people are perishing without Christ.

But in today's overstimulated world, many believers have lost that burden—not because they don't love God, but because they are drowning in noise, movement, and endless activity.

Distraction doesn't just steal time or delay action. It numbs the soul.

The Burden Is Birthed in Stillness

True burden is not birthed in a crowd or a meeting—it's birthed in the presence of God. When you sit with Him, hear His heart, and feel His passion for the lost, something shifts in you.

But most believers rarely get still enough to be burdened. Constant activity has become the enemy of conviction.

> **"Be still, and know that I am God…" —Psalm 46:10 (KJV)**

The burden for souls grows when we pause. When we see. When we weep.

Distraction keeps you in motion so you never stop long enough to feel what God feels. You keep moving, and the fire cools.

The Cost of a Numb Spirit

A numb spirit leads to:

- Indifference instead of intercession.
- Excuses instead of evangelism.
- Comfort instead of calling.
- Casual Christianity instead of kingdom urgency.

You may still go to church, serve, and sing, but without a burden, you're no longer reaching. You've stopped seeing lost people as lost. You've started tolerating what you were called to transform.

Signs That the Burden Has Faded

"Mine eye affecteth mine heart..." —Lamentations 3:51 (KJV)

The burden for souls is not merely a feeling—it is a fire. It's the holy ache that drives us to intercede, witness, and preach as though eternity is one breath away. But when that fire begins to dim, something dangerous happens: we get used to spiritual death.

We still go to church. We still say "amen." But we stop weeping. We stop noticing. And slowly, we drift from the urgency of the great commission into the routine of religion.

Below are five unmistakable signs that the burden has faded—and how to return to it.

1. You stop weeping over souls.

> **"They that sow in tears shall reap in joy. He that goeth forth and weepeth… shall doubtless come again with rejoicing…"** —Psalm 126:5–6 (KJV)

Tears are evidence that the heart is still tender. When your heart is aligned with heaven's, you cannot look at the lost and remain dry-eyed. The early church wept. The prophets wept. Jesus wept over Jerusalem.

When we stop weeping:

- We grow indifferent.
- We lose our sense of urgency.
- We forget what it cost Jesus to save us.

You may still preach, sing, and lead, but without tears, your labor is missing power.

Return Through:

- Praying for God to break your heart again.
- Reading scriptures about judgment and mercy.
- Sitting in silence and letting God restore your burden.

2. You stop noticing the spiritual needs of the people around you.

> **"But when he saw the multitudes, he was moved with compassion on them…"** —Matthew 9:36 (KJV)

Jesus saw what others ignored: the desperation in people's eyes, the hunger in their souls, the pain behind their smiles.

When the burden fades, you stop seeing. You walk by souls every day but never notice their eternal condition.

You stop thinking:

- "Do they know Christ?"
- "Are they hurting?"
- "Could I be the one to reach them?"

Spiritual blindness is a sign of a calloused heart.

Return Through:

- Asking God to open your eyes to the needs around you.
- Slowing down and listening when people speak.
- Intentionally engaging someone who is hurting or searching.

3. **Evangelism feels optional instead of essential.**

   "...woe is unto me, if I preach not the gospel!" —1 Corinthians 9:16 (KJV)

When the fire fades, the mission becomes negotiable. We see evangelism as a program, not a purpose. We say it's important, but it never becomes urgent. And eventually, it becomes nonexistent.

Reigniting the Fire of Soul Winning in Our Churches

You know the burden has faded when:

- You stop sharing your testimony.
- You make excuses about timing.
- You wait for "perfect opportunities" that never come.

The early church didn't treat evangelism as a task—it was their heartbeat.

Return Through:

- Asking the Holy Spirit to renew your zeal.
- Making soul winning a part of your daily life.
- Partnering with others to keep yourself accountable.

4. **You scroll past brokenness without praying.**

   "…and when he saw him, he had compassion…" —Luke 10:33 (KJV)

Today's world is full of digital brokenness. Every scroll reveals tragedy, grief, addiction, violence, and loss. But when the burden fades, we grow numb.

You see another overdose, another divorce, another crisis—and you feel nothing.

You stop praying. You stop caring. You keep scrolling.

That's not just distraction—it's spiritual desensitization.

Return Through:

- Committing to pray for at least one need every time you scroll.
- Turning off distractions and turning up intercession.
- Refusing to become comfortable with the pain you were called to heal.

5. You no longer say, "Lord, send me."

"Also I heard the voice of the Lord, saying, Whom shall I send, and who will go for us? Then said I, Here am I; send me." —Isaiah 6:8 (KJV)

Perhaps the clearest sign that the burden is gone is this: you've stopped volunteering.

— You no longer pray dangerous prayers.
— You no longer long to be used.
— You settle into spiritual maintenance mode.
— The fire has turned to smoke.
— Your call has grown cold.
— Your posture has become passive.

Return Through:

- Recommitting your life and time to God's purpose.
- Laying your fears and excuses on the altar.
- Saying "yes" to the next opportunity to serve, preach, or witness.

Don't Let the Flame Die

God's greatest grief is not when sinners sin—it's when the church forgets to care.

When we stop weeping, noticing, praying, reaching, and volunteering, we stop representing Jesus.

> **"I have somewhat against thee, because thou hast left thy first love." —Revelation 2:4 (KJV)**

But the good news is: you can come back.
The burden can return. The fire can fall again.
You just have to ask.

If these symptoms resonate with you, the burden hasn't disappeared—it's just been buried under distraction.

God Is Looking for Carriers of His Heart

> **"And I sought for a man among them, that should make up the hedge, and stand in the gap before me for the land, that I should not destroy it: but I found none." —Ezekiel 22:30 (KJV)**

God isn't just looking for performers—He's looking for intercessors, weepers, carriers of His burden for souls. Those who will walk the streets, go into the prisons, look into the eyes of the addicted, and see them the way He sees them: redeemable.

The burden is what separates the casual Christian from the compelled witness.

Reignite the Burden

If your heart has grown numb, you can be reignited. The Holy Spirit is still in the business of setting hearts on fire.

Here's how:

- **Pray dangerous prayers.** Ask God to break your heart for what breaks His.
- **Expose yourself to need.** Spend time with the hurting, the unsaved, the forgotten.
- **Study the lostness of humanity.** Let the Word and world open your eyes.
- **Worship deeply.** In God's presence, the fire is reignited.
- **Fast.** Silence your flesh to hear the cry of heaven again.

> "Is not this the fast that I have chosen… to undo heavy burdens…?" —Isaiah 58:6 (KJV)

The burden will return when your spirit gets quiet, and your heart becomes available.

The Urgency of the Hour

The world is not waiting for another conference, another production, or another brand of church. It's crying out for the real thing:

- A people who burn with God's fire.
- A church that preaches with authority.
- Believers who live with conviction.
- Voices that speak truth without shame.

Reigniting the Fire of Soul Winning in Our Churches

- Hands that reach the streets, not just the pews.

The harvest is still ripe (see John 4:35). But laborers are still few—not because they aren't available, but because many have become distracted, disunified, disinterested, or disobedient.

That must end now.

CHAPTER 28

EQUIPPING THE CHURCH TO OVERCOME AND RESTORE THE SOUL WINNING FIRE

Exposing the challenges is only the beginning. Now, the church must be equipped to rise above them and rediscover its first love—the mission to win souls. Restoring a culture of evangelism isn't about implementing trendy programs or forcing people into uncomfortable routines. It's about reigniting hearts, rebuilding priorities, and releasing the church back into its purpose.

This restoration begins with intentional equipping—biblically, practically, and spiritually.

Equip Through Sound Doctrine and Spirit-Filled Preaching

We cannot expect people to evangelize if they don't truly understand the message they carry. The church must return to bold, clear, uncompromised preaching of the gospel:

- The reality of sin and separation from God.
- The redemptive power of the cross.
- The necessity of repentance and new birth.

Reigniting the Fire of Soul Winning in Our Churches

- The urgency of eternity—heaven and hell are real.

When the Word is preached in truth and power, hearts are awakened, and passion for the lost is born again.

Key Action:

- Equip the church through regular gospel teaching and evangelism-centered series.
- Host doctrinal refreshers for leaders and believers who return to the foundation of salvation.

Equip Through Testimony and Personal Witness

One of the most powerful evangelism tools is your personal story. You don't need a stage or a mic—you just need a voice and a testimony. Equipping believers to share their story with boldness and clarity is a simple but impactful way to restore a soul winning culture.

Key Action:

- Offer testimony training workshops.
- Help believers craft their personal gospel testimony in 3–5 minutes.
- Encourage weekly "Testimony Sundays" or digital sharing challenges.

Equip Through Evangelism Training and Activation

The early church was empowered and sent. They weren't just filled with the Spirit—they were released into the harvest. Too often, believers are trained to serve inside the church, but not sent into the world.

We must train and activate the church in personal, relational, and public evangelism.

Key Action:

- Teach on evangelism styles: conversational, relational, service-based, street ministry, etc.
- Organize monthly outreach teams and soul winning missions in local communities.
- Provide practical role-playing scenarios to boost confidence.

Equip Through Prayer and Intercession

Before the church can evangelize with power, it must weep for the lost in prayer. Evangelism is spiritual warfare, and the altar must be re-established as a war room for souls.

Key Action:

- Launch intercessory prayer groups focused on unreached people, unsaved loved ones, and your city.
- Lead prayer nights where the names of lost individuals are called out before God.
- Teach how prayer precedes power and prepares hearts for the gospel.

Equip Through Discipleship and Follow-Up

Evangelism doesn't end at the altar—it begins there. Every soul that is won must be discipled, nurtured, and rooted in the Word. The church must be equipped not only to reach people, but to raise them into maturity.

Key Action:

- Develop follow-up systems for every new convert—calls, home visits, and spiritual mentorship.
- Pair new believers with trained disciple-makers.
- Teach the body how to walk with new believers through challenges, questions, and growth.

Equip Through Leadership and Lifestyle Modeling

Pastors and leaders must model what they want to multiply. If leadership is not passionate about soul winning, the congregation will not be either. Evangelism must become a visible value of church leadership.

Key Action:

- Encourage staff and elders to share testimonies, participate in outreach, and regularly win souls.
- Celebrate soul winning moments in leadership meetings and church services.
- Model soul winning as a lifestyle—not just a ministry department.

Equip Through Spirit-Empowered Living

We must teach the church that evangelism isn't done in human strength—it flows from a Spirit-filled life. The fire to witness comes through daily communion with the Holy Spirit, walking in boldness, discernment, and compassion.

Key Action:

- Teach on the role of the Holy Spirit in evangelism (see Acts 1:8).
- Lead believers through infilling, empowerment, and spiritual gifts training.
- Encourage ongoing dependency on the Spirit through fasting, prayer, and worship.

Releasing the Church into the Harvest

The church does not need more members—it needs more messengers. God is not just filling buildings—He is raising up burning ones, ready to carry the gospel into neighborhoods, nations, and next generations.

Equipping is not a one-time effort—it is a lifestyle of leadership that:

- Instructs in truth.
- Activates in power.
- Sends in love.
- Supports with prayer.
- Follows up with discipleship.

Reigniting the Fire of Soul Winning in Our Churches

The world is not waiting for perfection—it's waiting for the mobilized church.

Let us teach. Let us train. Let us equip. Then, let us send. And may the soul winning fire never go out again.

The Call to Rise

The time has come for the church to rise:

- Rise above comfort and return to consecration.
- Rise above compromise and walk in holiness.
- Rise above division and link arms for the harvest.
- Rise above silence and roar with truth and love.

The enemy isn't threatened by a casual church, but he fears a consecrated one. He fears the church that will break the mold, burn with purpose, and boldly declare, *"Here we are, Lord—send us!"*

— You are that church.
— You are that voice.
— You are that vessel.

Let the Fire Fall Again

This is not the time to play it safe. This is the time to carry the torch of evangelism with fresh fire. The church must refuse to be lukewarm, silent, or self-serving. Instead, it must become:

- Missional, not just motivational.
- Holy, not just helpful.
- Obedient, not just organized.

- Alive in the Spirit, not just active in programs.

Let us repent. Let us refocus. Let us return.

Because when the church rises above the challenge, the fire will fall, the harvest will be gathered, and heaven will rejoice.

CHAPTER 29

LET THE FIRE FALL AGAIN

"Will you not revive us again: that thy people may rejoice in thee?" —Psalm 85:6 (KJV)

There comes a time in the life of every generation when the church must decide who she will be: a flickering lamp of formality—or a blazing furnace of revival fire. That time is now. We are not called to maintain appearances—we are called to carry anointing. Not called to repeat cycles—but to reignite cities. The world doesn't need another motivational event. It needs a church that burns with heaven's flame.

This is not the time to play it safe. This is the time to let the fire fall again.

This Is Not the Time for Lukewarmness

"So then because thou art lukewarm... I will spue thee out of my mouth." —Revelation 3:16 (KJV)

Lukewarm Christianity is dangerous. It says the right things but does not carry power. It shows up to church but avoids the altar. It honors God with words, but not with fire.

Reigniting the Fire of Soul Winning in Our Churches

Lukewarmness:

- Tolerates sin.
- Delays obedience.
- Avoids sacrifice.
- Dims the urgency of evangelism.

But fire disturbs comfort. It stirs repentance. It demands change. The church must no longer apologize for burning with boldness—we must fan the flame.

This Is the Time to Be Missional, Not Just Motivational

"Go ye into all the world, and preach the gospel to every creature." —Mark 16:15 (KJV)

Motivational gatherings stir feelings. Missional movements save souls. The church was never called to impress—it was called to impact. We are not entertainers; we are messengers of eternity.

When fire falls:

- Services become sending stations.
- Every member becomes a missionary.
- The altar becomes a launching pad.
- The city becomes the mission field.

Programs don't win souls—burdened people do.

Pastor Dr. Claudine Benjamin

This Is the Time to Be Holy, Not Just Helpful

"Be ye holy; for I am holy." —1 Peter 1:16 (KJV)

Helpful churches serve communities, but holy churches transform them. Compassion without consecration is powerless. Holiness is not legalism—it's alignment with God's nature, authority, and power.

A holy church:

- Confronts sin.
- Walks in purity.
- Leads in humility.
- Hosts the presence of God.

Without holiness, there is no fire—only smoke.

> "The Lord, whom ye seek, shall suddenly come to his temple… and he shall purify…" —Malachi 3:1–3 (KJV)

We need a church that burns with both compassion and conviction.

This Is the Time to Be Obedient, Not Just Organized

"…to obey is better than sacrifice…" —1 Samuel 15:22 (KJV)

God is not impressed with excellent execution if there's no surrender. You can have the best branding, flawless systems, perfect rehearsals—but if the Spirit isn't leading, it's powerless.

Reigniting the Fire of Soul Winning in Our Churches

Obedience brings fire.

- When the apostles tarried in the upper room, the fire fell (see Acts 2).
- When Elijah built the altar in God's way, the fire fell (see 1 Kings 18).
- When the early church obeyed the command to go, miracles followed.

God won't anoint what we perform—He anoints what we obey.

This Is the Time to Be Alive in the Spirit, Not Just Active in Programs

"It is the spirit that quickeneth…" —John 6:63 (KJV)

Activity without anointing leads to burnout. Movement without the Spirit leads to man-made religion. The church must stop confusing busy calendars with spiritual fruit.

A Spirit-alive church is:

- Full of prayer and power.
- Marked by healing and prophecy.
- Led by the Spirit, not just preference.
- Yielded, not scripted.

"…where the Spirit of the Lord is, there is liberty." —2 Corinthians 3:17 (KJV)

The Spirit doesn't follow our schedule—He responds to surrender. It's time to let Him move again.

Pastor Dr. Claudine Benjamin

Let Us Repent. Let Us Refocus. Let Us Return.

> "Remember therefore from whence thou art fallen, and repent, and do the first works…" —Revelation 2:5 (KJV)

The path to revival is not complicated:

- Repent of where we've compromised.
- Refocus our attention on Jesus and the harvest.
- Return to the altar with hunger and humility.

This is a call to the church, not to change methods, but to recover the message.
Not to innovate more, but to intercede deeper.
Not to wait for better timing, but to cry out now.

When the Church Rises, the Fire Will Fall

> "And when the day of Pentecost was fully come… there came a sound from heaven as of a rushing mighty wind, and it filled all the house…" —Acts 2:1–2 (KJV)

When the church rises above the distractions, divisions, and distractions:

- The fire will fall.
- The harvest will be gathered.
- Heaven will rejoice.

This is not emotionalism. It's eternal urgency.
This is not hype. It's holy fire.

Reigniting the Fire of Soul Winning in Our Churches

This is not a suggestion. It's a summons.
Let the fire fall again.

The altar is waiting. The harvest is ready. The time is now. Let the church rise. Let the church burn. Let the church win.

Marks of a Church on Fire for the Harvest

1. It carries God's heart for the lost.

When the fire of God touches a church, the heart of the Father becomes the heartbeat of the people. They are burdened by the thought of souls going to hell. Their services are filled with urgency. Their prayers are marked by tears. The lost are not a category—they are a cause.

2. It prioritizes evangelism over entertainment.

A church on fire isn't trying to impress the world—it's trying to save it. It doesn't spend more on smoke machines than it does on outreach. It doesn't cater to consumer Christianity. It confronts sin with truth and calls people to the cross with boldness.

3. It operates in the power of the Holy Spirit.

The early church didn't have technology, but it had power. They laid hands on the sick, cast out demons, and preached with boldness. They weren't seeker-friendly—they were Spirit-filled. The fire of the Holy Ghost made them fearless.

That same fire is what we need now—not better sound systems, but burning hearts.

4. It disciples, not just converts.

A harvest of souls must be followed by a process of growth. A fire-filled church doesn't just make converts—it makes disciples. It nurtures, teaches, and trains new believers to walk in their purpose and reproduce themselves in others.

How the Fire Impacts the Community

When a church is truly on fire for the harvest:

- Crime drops because hearts are changed.
- Addiction rates fall because deliverance is happening.
- Families are restored because truth is preached.
- Revival spills into schools, businesses, and neighborhoods.

A church on fire becomes a city's greatest asset. It no longer waits for the lost to come in—it goes out and pulls them from the fire (see Jude 1:23).

How to Rekindle the Fire

If your church has lost the flame, it can be rekindled. God is not finished with your ministry. The same fire that fell at Pentecost can fall again.

1. Return to the upper room.

Make prayer and fasting the foundation again. Set aside time for corporate crying out to God. Invite the Spirit to burn away the flesh, routine, and religion.

2. Preach the uncompromised gospel.

No more diluted messages. Preach sin, the cross, repentance, the blood, and the reality of eternity. The gospel is still the power of God unto salvation (Romans 1:16).

3. Activate the people.

Every member is a minister. Train, equip, and send them out. Evangelism is not just for a department—it's for every disciple.

4. Ask for the fire.

God responds to desperation. Ask Him to send the fire again—to your pulpit, pews, parking lot, and city. Cry out like Elijah: **"Hear me, O Lord, hear me, that this people may know that thou art the Lord God, and that thou hast turned their heart back again." (1 Kings 18:37 - KJV).**

The Future Belongs to the Fiery Church

The churches that will thrive in the last days are not the trendiest or the biggest. They are the burning ones—the churches that are ablaze with love for Jesus and compassion for the lost.

God is not looking for polished presentations. He's looking for pure altars. He's not seeking applause. He's seeking obedience. He doesn't need showmanship. He needs surrendered vessels.

Let your church be one that makes hell nervous and heaven rejoice.

Final Call to the Church

If we don't burn, the world stays in darkness.
If we don't go, the lost stay unreached.
If we don't preach, people perish.
The time is now.
The harvest is ready.

Will your church burn again?

Father, set Your church on fire again. Remove complacency, entertainment, and compromise. Fill our altars, flood our pulpits, and fan the flame of evangelism in our hearts. Let us burn for You so brightly that the lost are drawn, the bound are set free, and the harvest is reaped. Ignite us again, Holy Spirit—in Jesus' name. Amen.

Declaration

We are a church on fire. We will not be cold, quiet, or compromised. We burn for souls. We burn for truth. We burn for revival. The fire is falling—and we say yes.

CHAPTER 30

CHURCH ACTIVATION CHECKLIST: REIGNITING THE FIRE FOR SOUL WINNING

Purpose

This checklist is designed to help pastors, leaders, and church members evaluate and activate their church's commitment to soul winning. Use it as a guide to refocus, re-engage, and reignite your church's evangelistic mission.

Spiritual Alignment

- Does our church regularly preach salvation, repentance, and eternity?
- Are altar calls and invitations to salvation clear and consistent?
- Are we teaching and equipping members to share their faith confidently?
- Do our leaders model personal evangelism?
- Is soul winning a central part of our church culture and vision?

Prayer and Intercession

- Do we have corporate prayer meetings focused on lost souls and revival?
- Are we praying by name for the unsaved in our families and communities?
- Have we designated intercessors or prayer teams to cover evangelism efforts?
- Do we fast regularly as a church body for a harvest of souls?

Outreach Initiatives

- Do we host regular community outreach events with a gospel focus?
- Are we actively evangelizing beyond the church walls (for example, street teams, door-to-door, online)?
- Do we have a presence in schools, prisons, shelters, or underserved areas?
- Are we offering practical resources (food, clothing, support) that open doors for ministry?
- Are we intentionally inviting and welcoming unbelievers to our services?

Discipleship and Follow-Up

- Do we have a clear process for discipling new converts?
- Are new believers being paired with mentors or spiritual guides?
- Are we offering baptism, foundational teaching, and spiritual growth opportunities?

- Do we follow up with visitors and those who respond to altar calls within 48 hours?

Evangelism Training

- Have we provided evangelism training workshops for our congregation?
- Are there resources available (tracts, conversation guides, Bibles)?
- Are youth and children being trained in age-appropriate evangelism?
- Do we celebrate and share testimonies of soul winning efforts?

Culture Shift and Accountability

- Is evangelism spoken about regularly from the pulpit?
- Do our church ministries (choir, ushers, media, etc.) carry the burden for souls?
- Are we setting evangelism goals and tracking progress?
- Are church members challenged to win at least one soul per month or year?
- Are we celebrating soul winning just as much as other ministry milestones?

Digital Evangelism

- Are we using our church's online platforms (social media, livestreams, website) to preach the gospel?
- Do we offer short gospel clips, testimonies, or salvation prayers online?

- Do we encourage members to share their testimonies or invite others digitally?

Leadership Responsibility

- Are our pastors and leaders actively involved in soul winning efforts?
- Have we established a dedicated evangelism team or department?
- Are leaders mentoring others to multiply outreach?

Activation Challenge

- Host a Harvest Revival Weekend with a focus on soul winning.
- Launch a 30-Day Evangelism Challenge for your congregation.
- Identify five souls to pray for and intentionally witness to this month.
- Appoint a Harvest Coordinator to oversee evangelistic outreach and follow-up.

If our church closed tomorrow, would the lost in our community notice?

Would they miss the fire, the message, the outreach, the invitation to know Jesus?

Let us be a church so active in the harvest that hell trembles every time our doors open.

CONCLUSION

UNTIL THE WHOLE WORLD HEARS

> "And this gospel of the kingdom shall be preached in all the world for a witness unto all nations; and then shall the end come." —Matthew 24:14 (KJV)

The mission is not finished. The gospel has not yet been preached to every person. The fields are still white. The lost are still waiting. And the call from heaven still echoes to the church: Go. Compel them. Reach them. Win them.

This is not the conclusion of a book—it's the continuation of a commission.

The Flame Must Keep Burning

Everything we've discussed throughout this book—vision, equipping, boldness, compassion, leadership, and structure—has one goal: that your church would burn with a holy fire for souls that never dies out.

> "The fire shall ever be burning upon the altar; it shall never go out." —Leviticus 6:13 (KJV)

Churches were never meant to be monuments. They are meant to be missional centers, sending believers into neighborhoods, schools, workplaces, and nations with the saving power of the gospel.

This is the fire we must tend. This is the fire we must pass on.

We Are Accountable for the Harvest

The church will not be judged by how large it became, but by how faithful it was to its assignment.

> **"Son of man, I have made thee a watchman unto the house of Israel: therefore hear the word at my mouth, and give them warning from me. When I say unto the wicked, Thou shalt surely die; and thou givest him not warning, nor speakest to warn the wicked from his wicked way, to save his life; the same wicked man shall die in his iniquity; but his blood will I require at thine hand." —Ezekiel 3:17–18 (KJV)**

We must weep again. We must witness again. We must live like souls depend on it—because they do.

The Lost Are Still Waiting

In your city/town/community, there are:

- Fathers bound by addiction.
- Teenagers contemplating suicide.
- Single mothers overwhelmed with shame.
- Elderly people dying without Christ.

- Entire families are one encounter away from transformation.

"How then shall they call on him in whom they have not believed? and how shall they believe… without a preacher?" —Romans 10:14 (KJV)

They will not believe unless someone tells them. That someone is you.

One Church Can Make a Difference

Don't wait for a movement—become one. Don't wait for permission—God already gave it. Don't wait until everything is perfect—go with what you have.

Let your church be the place where:

- Lost people are regularly saved.
- Disciples are made and sent.
- Outreach is prioritized and celebrated.
- The fire never dies.

Until the Whole World Hears

The gospel is still the power of God unto salvation (see Romans 1:16). The church is still God's chosen vessel. The harvest is still ready. And Jesus is still coming.

Until the whole world hears:

- We will preach.

Reigniting the Fire of Soul Winning in Our Churches

- We will go.
- We will give.
- We will train.
- We will burn.

This is not a side mission. It is the central call of the church.

Let this be said of your church: **"That's the place where the fire for souls still burns."**

A Call to the Church Today

We declare that the church is awakening from slumber. We will not be silent, distracted, or disengaged. We return to the altar, to the mission, and to the fire. We will not settle for religious form—we will pursue the fullness of God's power. The harvest will not be ignored. Our hearts will burn again. We are a church on fire, fearless in our witness, and faithful to the mission of Jesus Christ. Revival starts with us. Let the fire fall, and let it spread.

> **"Therefore let us not sleep, as do others; but let us watch and be sober."** —1 Thessalonians 5:6 (KJV)

We are not waiting for a revival. We are the revival God is waiting for. The time for silence, slumber, and spiritual disengagement is over. There is a cry from heaven echoing across the earth—a call for the church to wake up, rise up, and burn again.

This is not a season for cosmetic Christianity. This is not the hour for performance-driven gatherings. This is the time for a church that is fueled by the Spirit, formed at the altar, and focused on the harvest.

We Will Not Be Silent

**"Cry aloud, spare not, lift up thy voice like a trumpet…"
—Isaiah 58:1 (KJV)**

The church must regain her voice. We are not echo chambers of culture—we are the voice of heaven on earth. When the church is silent, darkness advances. But when the church speaks, hell trembles.

We will not be silent about:

- Sin and righteousness.
- The reality of hell and the hope of heaven.
- The urgency of salvation.
- The call to repentance.

The days of whispering truth to avoid offense are over. We will preach the gospel with boldness, love, and fire.

We Will Not Be Distracted

"No man that warreth entangleth himself with the affairs of this life…" —2 Timothy 2:4 (KJV)

The harvest is too urgent for the church to be caught in carnality. We've been distracted by trends, platforms, entertainment, and convenience. But today, we shake off the dust of distraction and fix our eyes on eternal purpose.

Reigniting the Fire of Soul Winning in Our Churches

We return to:

- The simplicity of the gospel.
- The priority of soul winning.
- The centrality of the cross.
- The burden for the lost.

We refuse to be a church that scrolls while souls perish.

We Will Not Be Disengaged

"And I sought for a man among them... but I found none." —Ezekiel 22:30 (KJV)

The days of passive Christianity are over. Every believer is called. Every laborer is needed. We cannot sit on the sidelines while nations collapse into darkness. We will engage with urgency and compassion.

Disengagement looks like:

- Praying casually.
- Witnessing occasionally.
- Worshipping emotionally but living carnally.
- Having church without being the church.

But we are waking up. We are taking our place. We are reengaging with heaven's mandate.

Pastor Dr. Claudine Benjamin

We Return to the Altar

> **"And the fire upon the altar shall be burning in it; it shall not be put out…" —Leviticus 6:12 (KJV)**

The altar is where the fire falls. It's where the flesh dies and the Spirit takes over. For too long, we've built stages but abandoned the altar. We've organized services but failed to host the presence of God.

Now we return to:

- Altars of repentance.
- Altars of prayer.
- Altars of surrender.
- Altars where the glory of God invades again.

Let our churches be marked not by how fast we finish, but by how long we linger.

We Return to the Mission

> **"Go ye into all the world, and preach the gospel to every creature." —Mark 16:15 (KJV)**

The great commission is not a suggestion. It's not optional. It is the mandate of every church and every believer. The mission has not changed—but many of us have.

We've traded mission for maintenance. Evangelism for entertainment. Discipleship for digital content. But now we return to what Jesus died for: souls.

Reigniting the Fire of Soul Winning in Our Churches

We will:

- Preach again.
- Reach again.
- Go again.
- Disciple again.

We will win the lost or we will lose our fire.

We Return to the Fire

"...he shall baptize you with the Holy Ghost, and with fire." —Matthew 3:11 (KJV)

Fire is not a feeling—it is the evidence of God's presence. The early church was birthed in fire, sustained by fire, and advanced by fire. That fire purified, empowered, emboldened, and multiplied them.

We must reject:

- Lukewarm living.
- Comfortable Christianity.
- Powerless religion.
- Casual compromise.

And return to:

- Holy desperation.
- Spirit-led services.
- Risk-taking obedience.
- Holy Ghost boldness.

Let the church burn again. Let the altars blaze. Let every heart be set aflame with holy urgency.

The Harvest Will Not Be Ignored

"Say not ye, There are yet four months… lift up your eyes, and look on the fields…" —John 4:35 (KJV)

The harvest is ready. The fields are white. The souls are searching. But the church has been sleeping. No more. We declare that the harvest will not be ignored.

We will:

- See the lost again.
- Weep over the broken again.
- Preach the cross again.
- Do the work again.

Let us stop measuring ministry by size, popularity, or applause. Let us measure it by how many lives are rescued from hell.

We Are a Church on Fire

We are not a church content with survival. We are a church called to revival.
We are not fearful—we are faithful.
We are not shrinking back—we are stepping forward.

We are:

- A church on fire.

Reigniting the Fire of Soul Winning in Our Churches

- A church with vision.
- A church with power.
- A church with a voice.

Revival Starts With Us

We declare that:

- The slumber is breaking.
- The fire is rising.
- The call is clear.
- The Spirit is stirring.

We will not wait for another move. We are the move.
We will not wait for others to rise. We are rising.
Revival starts with us. Let the fire fall, and let it spread.

REFLECTION GUIDE

A CALL TO THE CHURCH TODAY

Personal Reflection Questions

1. Have I allowed anything to distract me from the mission of soul winning?

2. When was the last time I lingered at the altar in surrender?

3. Am I burning with spiritual fire, or just going through religious motions?

Scriptures for Meditation

- Revelation 2:4–5
- Luke 24:32
- Mark 16:15
- Leviticus 6:13

Practical Actions This Week

1. Set aside time to pray specifically for one lost soul by name.

2. Attend a church service or create a prayer space where you allow God to speak and stir you.

3. Share the gospel or your testimony with one person, even if it's uncomfortable.

SCRIPTURE REFERENCE INDEX

Organized by key themes from the book for teaching, preaching, and study.

The Great Commission and Mandate

- Matthew 28:19–20
- Mark 16:15
- Luke 24:47–48
- John 20:21
- Acts 1:8

The Heart of God for the Lost

- Luke 19:10
- Ezekiel 33:11
- 2 Peter 3:9
- John 3:16–17
- Luke 15:4–7

Urgency and Readiness

- John 4:35
- Romans 13:11
- Proverbs 10:5
- 2 Corinthians 6:2
- Matthew 24:14

Boldness and Power for Witnessing

- Acts 4:29–31
- 2 Timothy 1:6–7
- Proverbs 28:1
- Ephesians 6:19–20
- 1 Peter 3:15

Evangelism as a Lifestyle

- Matthew 5:14–16
- Romans 10:14–15
- Colossians 4:5–6
- 2 Corinthians 5:18–20
- 1 Thessalonians 1:8

The Cost of Silence

- Ezekiel 3:17–19
- Revelation 3:15–16
- Isaiah 5:20
- 2 Timothy 4:2–5
- Matthew 25:46

Multiplication and Discipleship

- 2 Timothy 2:2
- Matthew 28:20
- Luke 6:40
- Acts 2:41–47
- John 15:16

www.ingramcontent.com/pod-product-compliance
Lightning Source LLC
Chambersburg PA
CBHW070720160426
43192CB00009B/1255